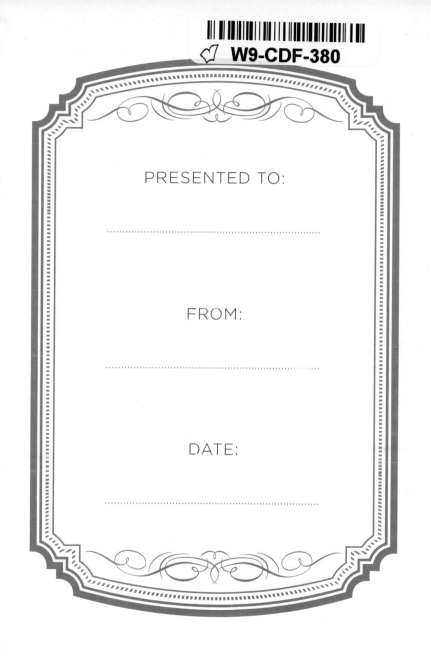

PRESENTED TO:

....

FROM:

....

DATE:

....

THE
Promise
CODE

40 Bible Promises
Every Believer
Should Claim

O. S. Hawkins

COUNTRYMAN®
An Imprint of Thomas Nelson Publishers

THOMAS NELSON
Since 1798

Published in Nashville, Tennessee, by Thomas Nelson. Thomas Nelson is a registered trademark of HarperCollins Christian Publishing, Inc.

Thomas Nelson titles may be purchased in bulk for educational, business, fund-raising, or sales promotional use. For information, please email SpecialMarkets@ThomasNelson.com.

Cover design by Bruce DeRoos, Left Coast Design, LLC
Interior design by Kristy L. Edwards

ISBN 978-1-4002-3527-8 (audiobook)
ISBN 978-1-4002-3525-4 (eBook)
ISBN 978-1-4002-3524-7 (HC)

Printed in China

22 23 24 25 26 AMY 10 9 8 7 6 5 4 3 2 1

CONTENTS

INTRODUCTION

*P*romises made are always appreciated. But promises kept are what mean the most. It is one thing to make a promise and quite another to keep it. Every one of us can attest to the validity of that truth. We all have had our own experiences of promises that were made and never kept. However, there is someone to whom this does not apply. Did you know that the Bible is replete with promises God has made . . . to *you* . . . and that He has a perfect record of keeping all His promises?

Though we are good at making promises, we often become lax when it comes to keeping them. But this never happens with God. Whether we keep our promises or not is based on the content of our character. An unrepentant, repeat thief may appear before a judge and promise never to steal again. But his trustworthiness, based on his past recurring behavior, does not attest to his sincerity. Because of the thief's lack of character and trustworthiness, a judge would never declare such a man innocent. So, how can we trust God and the promises He has made to us? Because of His character and the fact that the Bible declares that it is "impossible for God to lie" (Hebrews 6:18). His Word is His bond. Your Bible is laced on every page with promises He has made to you—promises He wants you to claim as your very own. It is one thing to read the Bible and struggle with its precepts and quite another thing to believe the Bible and stand on its promises.

One thing I learned early on in my own Christian experience is that in the kingdom of God we do not live by explanations; we live by promises. Do you remember Naaman, the commander of the king's armies of Syria? He contracted leprosy and searched out every medical specialist providing every possible cure that could be found, but to no avail. In a desperate, last-ditch attempt, he approached the prophet Elisha. The man of God gave him instructions to go to the Jordan River and immerse himself seven times with the promise that he would then be cured.

Infuriated by what he considered an absurdity, Naaman got back in his chariot and sped away. However, he was fortunate enough to have a servant with him who pointed out the truth that he had nothing to lose. So the proud conqueror approached the Jordan River, took off his royal robes, and submerged himself seven times. When he emerged after the seventh dip, the Bible records, "his flesh was restored like the flesh of a little child, and he was clean" (2 Kings 5:14). Naaman obeyed the promise and found his cure. But, like some of us, he almost missed the opportunity for healing because he was looking for an explanation—when God had

given him a promise. In God's kingdom we do not live by explanations, we live by Bible promises.

The Promise Code is designed to lead you into a new lifestyle of trusting in, and living by, the promises of God. This is how we live the faith life. The Bible declares that "faith comes by hearing, and hearing by the word of God"

> In God's kingdom we do not live by explanations; we live by Bible promises.

(Romans 10:17). Finding God's promise to you in His Word and standing on it is what produces your own faith, the kind of faith God says can still move mountains (Matthew 17:20).

A few of God's promises to us are unconditional, not based on anything we might do or not do. One such promise is found in the sign of the rainbow signifying God's pledge to never destroy the world again by a flood (Genesis 9:13–16). However, most of God's promises to you and to me are conditional. He promises to "forgive us our sins." But in the same verse, there is an "if." "If we confess our sins, He is faithful and just to forgive us our sins and to cleanse us from all unrighteousness" (1 John 1:9). Many of God's promises are prefaced with an "if," which is followed by a "then." We see this in one of the most repeated of God's promises: "*If* My people who are called by My name will humble themselves, and pray and seek My face, and turn from their wicked ways,

then I will hear from heaven, and will forgive their sin and heal their land" (2 Chronicles 7:14, emphasis added).

Throughout centuries of the Christian experience, the promises of God have sustained His people. When all hope seemed lost, believers have held to the promises of God. If there was ever a day the family of God needed to leave their explanations behind and cling to the promises of God's Word, it is today.

Let's begin the journey of discovering forty of the most precious promises in the Bible, coming to an understanding of what is behind them, and then claiming them for our very own. But let me be clear: you don't find a Bible promise. It is not like playing Russian roulette with the Word of God by simply opening your Bible, closing your eyes, and letting your finger fall on a particular verse to claim. No, you don't find a Bible promise. Bible promises find you! In the normal traffic pattern of your daily Bible reading, God has His way of reaching down by His Spirit and quickening a verse to your heart so you know that it is His special promise just to you—in your own snapshot in time—and right at the point of your particular need. So, let's turn the page and begin the great adventure of unlocking the Promise Code and living our lives by the promises of God's Word.

1 THE PROMISE OF A BRIGHTER TOMORROW

We know that all things work together for good to those who love
God, to those who are the called according to His purpose.
—ROMANS 8:28

No volume on the precious promises of God would be complete without mention of the one that has, perhaps, brought more hope to believers and the one that has so often sustained our faith as we have attempted to navigate our way through various difficult seasons of life. That, of course, would be found here in the words of Paul to the Romans. This is the one verse on which I have personally climbed atop and taken my stand, finding refuge and hope in times of confusion and need.

THE PROMISE IS CONSTRUCTIVE IN ITS APPEAL

As we dissect the elements of this powerful and very personal promise, we immediately note that it is *constructive in its appeal*. Paul assured us that "things work together." This is one of the most comforting thoughts in all Scripture; things that come our way in life have a supernatural way of working together for our good. They can be constructive in

nature. As you look back over your own faith journey, consider the events that, in the moment, seemed disastrous yet had a way of actually working out for good. This verse is a reminder that God Himself is behind the scenes in our lives, and things have their own way—not by accident or by blind chance—of working together for our good.

In the language of the New Testament, one Greek word translates this entire phrase, "things work together." The word is *synergia*, and we derive our English word *synergy* from it. A constructive and synergistic principle is at work in our lives. This certainly does not mean that everything that comes our way is good. In fact, many of us are confronted with issues that are downright bad and painful. You may be faced with financial setbacks, sickness, disappointment, and so on. However, this verse assures us that God can take our mistakes, messes, and misfortunes and work them together for our good and His glory.

God can take our mistakes, messes, and misfortunes and work them together for our good and His glory.

King David captured this truth and recorded these poignant words for posterity: "It is good for me that I have been afflicted, that I may learn Your statutes" (Psalm 119:71).

THE PROMISE IS COMPREHENSIVE
IN ITS APPROACH

Not only is this promise constructive in its appeal, it is *comprehensive in its approach*. The promise says, *"All things* work together for good." When I meditate on this promise, I am prone to ask myself if I can really believe it. Had Paul said "some things" or "many things" or even "most things" it would be a bit more palatable. But "all things"? *All things* can include unfair things. This was certainly true for Joseph, who was sold into slavery, taken to a foreign land, falsely accused of a crime, and thrown into an Egyptian dungeon. Also, consider the one from whom these words flowed. Paul was shipwrecked at Malta, stoned at Lystra and left for dead, and repeatedly beaten and berated during the years of his missionary journeys. For Paul, these words were not simply trite platitudes but were issued out of his own personal experience as the Holy Spirit led him to record this promise.

Yes, *all things* are what? *Working together.* For what? *Our good.* All things—not in isolation, not necessarily in and of themselves, but when worked together in the tapestry of the cross—have a way of coming out on the other end for our good. This promise is comprehensive, not just constructive.

THE PROMISE IS CONDITIONAL IN ITS APPLICATION

However, before you claim it as your own, look closer. This promise is *conditional in its application*. It is given exclusively to "those who love God, to those who are the called according to His purpose." It is not for everyone. This is not a blanket, unconditional promise. It is for those who "love God." Only those who love Him and sense that there is a purpose in their lives can understand the deep truth of Romans 8:28. And when they do, they can say with Job, "Naked I came from my mother's womb, and naked shall I return there. The LORD gave, and the LORD has taken away; blessed be the name of the LORD" (Job 1:21).

Love is something you do. In the Bible love is always equated with action. "For God so loved the world . . . that He gave" (John 3:16). He did something. Jesus said, "If you love Me, keep My commandments" (John 14:15). John framed it thus: "For this is the love of God, that we keep His commandments" (1 John 5:3). Loving God and abiding in His will "according to His purpose" is the condition by which the truth of this promise comes home to our hearts.

> Love is something you do. In the Bible love is always equated with action.

There is one final thought. Don't leave out the first phrase of this promise. It begins with "We know. . . ." Note carefully the plural pronoun at play: "we." Yes, *we* know. This promise was never intended to be understood by the world. It is a foreign language to those outside Christ. It is, in its essence, a family secret for those of us in the family of God. The promise found in Romans 8:28 is something that *we* know that those who are not part of God's forever family cannot comprehend. But we can. Yes, "We know that . . . all things . . . work together for good—to those who love God, to those who are the called according to His purpose."

The next time you feel overwhelmed by situations or circumstances swirling around you that seem beyond your control, climb up on this Bible promise. Stand there. Believe it. Claim it as your very own.

————— A PROMISE AND A PRAYER —————

The Lord will perfect that which concerns me;
Your mercy, O Lord, endures forever.
Psalm 138:8

Lord, in the midst of the storm, help me to hold fast to Your promise that "all things are working together" for my good and, most importantly, for Your glory. In Jesus' name, amen.

2   THE PROMISE OF HIS ALL-SUFFICIENT GRACE

*"My grace is sufficient for you, for My strength
is made perfect in weakness."*

—2 CORINTHIANS 12:9

*N*one of us are immune to disappointments and defeats, heartaches and heartbreaks, struggles and setbacks. These trials will affect each of us at one time or another. In fact, behind some of the most radiant lives I have known have been some of the biggest challenges. The great apostle Paul attested to this fact in his second letter to the Corinthians. He had a problem, and he had asked the Lord on three different occasions to remove it. Yet it was still there. This same man who had written to the Romans saying, "We are more than conquerors through Him who has loved us" (Romans 8:37), this same man who had said, "All things work together for good" (Romans 8:28), laid bare his heart in admission that he had a situation in which he could find no relief.

THE PROBLEM

His explanation began with *a problem*. He referred to his problem as "a thorn in the flesh" (2 Corinthians 12:7). What this "thorn" actually was no one knows for sure. But it was something physical in nature. It was a thorn in the "flesh." Some have speculated it was his physical appearance. After all, "his bodily presence [was] weak" (2 Corinthians 10:10). He had been lashed with a Roman whip almost two hundred times, he had been stoned at least three times—and once left for dead—and virtually every bone in his body had been fractured. Others contend his "thorn" was epilepsy. Still others speculate it was his failing eyesight, for earlier he had written to the Galatians saying, "See with what large letters I have written to you with my own hand!" (6:11). He had stated to them that he was confident that "if possible, you would have plucked out your own eyes and given them to me" (Galatians 4:15). Whatever it was, it was so irritating to him that he saw it as a problem and as an impediment to his work.

THE PURPOSE

But behind it all was *a purpose*. He had asked the Lord not once, not twice, but three times to remove it from him. But God did not remove it, for He had a greater purpose in it. Consider Paul's words: "Lest I should be exalted above measure by the abundance of the revelations, a thorn in the flesh was given to me" (2 Corinthians 12:7). Paul knew that this problem was "given" to him by God. God had big plans for

> Paul knew that this problem was "given" to him by God.

Paul. He later went from this experience to take the gospel to the entire Mediterranean world and ended up giving us half our New Testament through his own pen.

Haven't most of us been there, having something, or someone, who becomes a "thorn" in our own flesh? Perhaps, like Paul, we have asked the Lord repeatedly to free us from the problem only to find that it had been "given to us" by the Lord Himself to keep us humble and to fulfill His own purpose in our lives. Paul realized there was a divine purpose in his debilitating problem, and primarily it was to keep him from a sense of self-importance and self-exaltation.

THE PROMISE

Even though God did not answer Paul as he had hoped, He did something better. He gave him *a promise*: "He said to me, 'My grace is sufficient for you, for My strength is made perfect in weakness'" (2 Corinthians 12:9). God's grace is always enough—more than enough—for whatever need we may face. After all, grace is best defined as getting what we do not deserve. This is what distinguishes grace from mercy. Mercy is not getting what we do deserve. God is rich in grace and showers us daily with blessings we do not deserve. Earlier in the Corinthian letter Paul had said, "For you know the grace of our Lord Jesus Christ, that though He was rich, yet for your sakes He became poor, that you through His poverty might become rich" (2 Corinthians 8:9).

Perhaps even as you read these words, your own heart is heavy, and you have your own "thorn in the flesh" distracting you. In his epistle in the New Testament, James reminded us that "He [God] gives more grace . . . God resists the proud, but gives grace to the humble" (James 4:6). Whoever you are, whatever your circumstance, wherever you may reside, and with whomever you may have conflict, you can rest and rely on the promise that God's grace is sufficient.

THE POSSIBILITY

Finally, Paul left us with *a possibility* of much-needed strength that can actually come from weakness. We do not have to be strong. We can be weak, and in our own weakness we can find supernatural strength to meet the challenges of the day. Paul moved from being obsessed with his problem, asking the Lord repeatedly to take it away to no avail, to saying, "Therefore most gladly I will rather boast in my infirmities, that the power of Christ may rest upon me. . . . For when I am weak, then I am strong" (2 Corinthians 12:9–10).

There is a strange kinship between

> We can be weak, and in our own weakness we can find supernatural strength to meet the challenges of the day.

Paul's thorns and the thorns that pierced the brow of our Lord. Jesus, in weakness, with thorns in His brow and spikes nailed through His hands and feet, became strong. Could it be that every time Paul sensed the pressure of his thorn it reminded him of the power of the cross? There is nothing lovely about a crown of thorns. There may be nothing lovely about the thorn that irritates you. The cross was a cruel and harsh thing. Your thorn may be all of that to you. But before we turn the page to the next chapter, there is a final word to add. Paul said of his thorn that it "was given to me" (2 Corinthians 12:7). Make sure you are not trying to rid yourself of the very thing God "has given" you for His own purpose in your life. Then, stand on His promise: "My grace is sufficient for you."

A PROMISE AND A PRAYER

God is able to make all grace abound toward you,
that you, always having all sufficiency in all things,
may have an abundance for every good work.
2 CORINTHIANS 9:8

Lord, Your love has no limit, Your grace has no measure. You are all I need, always and in all ways. Your grace is sufficient for me. In Jesus' name, amen.

3   THE PROMISE OF
A GRACE GIFT

For by grace you have been saved through faith, and
that not of yourselves; it is the gift of God.

—EPHESIANS 2:8

*G*ift giving and gift receiving are important parts of
our own experiences. When birthdays and anniver-
saries roll around each year, we engage in this traditional
pastime. The Bible teaches that when it comes time for gifts,
"it is more blessed to give than to receive" (Acts 20:35). The
Lord should know. After all, He has given us our greatest
gift: "The gift of God is eternal life in Christ Jesus our Lord"
(Romans 6:23).

All the Bible writers were careful to describe eternal
life as a free gift and not something that could be earned or
deserved. To a Samaritan woman at a well, Jesus declared,
"If you knew the gift of God, and who it is who says to you,
'Give Me a drink,' you would have asked Him, and He would
have given you living water" (John 4:10). Peter called for
repentance on the Day of Pentecost with the promise to his
hearers that, "you shall receive the gift of the Holy Spirit"
(Acts 2:38). James added, "Every good gift and every perfect gift is from above" (James 1:17). And Paul summed it all

11

up, saying, "Thanks be to God for His indescribable gift!" (2 Corinthians 9:15).

In the Bible promise of this chapter, Paul made plain that a gift has three characteristics. A gift is costly. It costs the giver something to give it. A gift is conditional. It is of no use unless it is received by the one to whom it is intended. And a gift is calculated. Behind the giving of a gift is the desire to benefit and bless the recipient.

GIFTS ARE COSTLY

When we give a gift, it costs us something to do so. But no gift ever cost as much as God's gift of eternal life. Paul, in our promise, said, "By grace you have been saved," making plain that the origin of our salvation is found in Him and not in us or any of our human efforts. Salvation is God's work, provided by His grace, and is not offered in response to any good thing we may have done. It is provided to us wholly because of His grace.

Grace is God's unmerited and underserved favor toward us. It came at a great price. The Father did not send Jesus to die on the cross to provide the gift of our salvation for us because we kept begging and pleading with Him to do so. It was by His grace alone. Grace can be defined as getting what we don't deserve. No wonder we call it "amazing." God's gift to us came at a high cost, the sacrificial and substitutionary death of His only Son on the cross. Gifts cost us something.

GIFTS ARE CONDITIONAL

What good is a gift you pick out and purchase for someone if they refuse to receive it? Listen to our promise; this

> Grace can be defined as getting what we don't deserve. No wonder we call it "amazing."

gift is received "through faith." That is it. The gift of God's grace is conditional on our transferring our faith to Christ alone for our salvation. These words make me want to shout this verse: "Through faith . . . not of yourselves . . . the gift of God!" The following verse attests that it is not of works "lest anyone should boast" (Ephesians 2:9). Our faith is the channel through which salvation flows from God to us. It is *through* faith.

Paul's repetition of the truth that salvation is "not of ourselves" and "not of works" brings emphasis to his point that it is the "gift of God." In some other faiths, people do extreme things—even give their lives—in feeble attempts to please their gods and be ushered into heaven. But it is "by grace . . . through faith . . . not of yourselves; it is the gift of God." God is offering His free gift of eternal life to any and all who will simply believe by faith in Christ alone.

What should amaze us is that although God is offering by His grace this free gift, we still have to encourage and

exhort people to receive it. Salvation is God's work (by grace) in God's way (through faith). Gift giving is costly. But it is also conditional.

GIFTS ARE CALCULATED

Why do you and I give gifts to those we love? It is because we calculate the fact that it will benefit and bless the one who receives it. Otherwise, why bother? It is the same with God's gift to us. He gives us salvation to benefit us and to bless us. Paul continued with this promise to say, "For we are His workmanship, created in Christ Jesus for good works, which God prepared beforehand that we should walk in them" (Ephesians 2:10).

When you receive God's gift of eternal life through faith, you become a new creation, "created in Christ Jesus." You become His "workmanship." We derive our English word *poem* from a transliteration of this Greek word. *You* are God's own creation, His own work of art. He so fashioned and formed you that no one else has your specific DNA. You are unique and indescribably valuable to Him.

> *You* are God's own creation, His own work of art.

Think about this the next time you sit around your Christmas tree with your extended family, exchanging gifts. Don't watch the face of the one opening the gift. Catch a glimpse of the joy on the face of the giver as he or she watches the one they love open the gift. And so it is with God. His gift to us was costly. It is conditional. And it is calculated—to benefit and bless you. Claim this promise—and receive it gladly—through faith.

—————— A PROMISE AND A PRAYER ——————

If anyone is in Christ, he is a new creation; old things have passed away; behold, all things have become new.
2 CORINTHIANS 5:17

Lord, what more can be said than to join Paul in saying, "Thanks be to God for His indescribable gift"? What a benefit—what a blessing to know You, whom to know is life, not just abundant but eternal. In Jesus' name, amen.

4 THE PROMISE OF ETERNAL SECURITY

"My sheep hear My voice, and I know them, and they follow Me. And I give them eternal life, and they shall never perish; neither shall anyone snatch them out of My hand."

—JOHN 10:27–28

*L*aced throughout the verses of the tenth chapter of John's gospel are promises to us from our Lord related to how He cares for us like a shepherd cares for his own sheep. These words of Jesus are packed with principles and promises. He knows us—everything about us—past, present, and future. He gives us eternal life, the greatest of all gifts. He promises that we shall never perish. And He reminds us that we are securely held in His strong hand, so much so that nothing and no one can snatch us from His grasp.

This analogy of the shepherd and his sheep is not unique to the New Testament. Many millions through the ages have heard these words of the psalmist King David: "The LORD is my Shepherd" (Psalm 23:1). Along with the familiar John 3:16, these are the words whispered by many a soldier in a foxhole on a foreign battlefield on some star-filled night. These words of promise are the syllables often formed by the chapped lips of dying saints on their deathbeds of affliction: "The LORD is my Shepherd."

David was not always a king. He got his start in the shepherds' fields of Bethlehem, tending sheep. Only a real shepherd could have penned the words we find in the six short verses of Psalm 23. In fact, the first five words—"The LORD is my shepherd"—hold the key to understanding Jesus' use of the shepherd-sheep analogy.

THE LORD IS PREEMINENT

The Bible does not say, "A Lord is my shepherd." It says, "*The* LORD is my shepherd." He is *preeminent*. There is no other Lord. He has no peer. His is the name that is "above every name" (Philippians 2:9). Our Good Shepherd stands alone above all others. The word translated *Lord* in Psalm 23:1 is the Hebrew word *Yahweh*. The Jews regard this name as so holy they will not even speak of it audibly or write it on paper.

> Our Good Shepherd stands alone above all others.

Only God's record book in heaven has recorded how many martyrs of the church went to their deaths and laid down their lives because they insisted on these two words: "The Lord." In the early church, they would neither bow nor bend to confess that Caesar was Lord. They gave their lives

because they were convinced there was only one Lord, and His sweet name is Jesus.

THE LORD IS PRESENT

But that is not all. David continued, "The LORD *is* my shepherd." He is not only preeminent, He is *present*. This is not past tense. He did not say, "The Lord was my shepherd." It is not future tense. He did not say, "The Lord will be my shepherd." This promise is for you and me right now. He *is* our Shepherd. He is with you to meet whatever need you may have this very moment as you read these words.

Moses was another Bible shepherd who found himself one day tending sheep on the back side of a desert when God began to speak to him from a burning bush. Upon receiving instructions to return to Egypt to be the great emancipator of the Jews, he inquired about who he should say had sent him to lead such a task. God replied, "I AM WHO I AM. . . . Thus you shall say . . . 'I AM has sent me to you'" (Exodus 3:14). He is the Great I AM . . . not the Great I WAS, or the Great I WILL BE. No wonder David said, "The LORD *is* my shepherd." And no wonder Jesus often repeated, "I *am* the Good Shepherd."

THE LORD IS PERSONAL

Next comes the promise that He is *personal*. David did not say, "The Lord is a shepherd." No! Look closely. "The LORD is

my shepherd." That little two-letter, one-syllable possessive pronoun, *my*, makes a huge difference to life's circumstances and situations. We may get word that someone's little child is deathly sick, and we have compassion and feel sorrow. But

> This is not just any shepherd. This is personal. This is *my* Shepherd.

what a difference it would make if it were *my* child. This is not just any shepherd. This is personal. This is *my* Shepherd.

The awesome discovery that the God of this universe and of all created order is concerned about me personally gives purpose and meaning to my short sojourn on this speck of a planet in His vast expanse. Unfortunately, however, not everyone can say this and claim this promise. Jesus said "My sheep hear My voice, and I know them, and they follow Me. And I give them eternal life" (John 10:27–28). Christ's sheep know His voice, and they follow Him. He is personal. He is *my* Shepherd.

THE LORD IS PROTECTIVE

One thousand years after King David wrote this psalm, One appeared on the scene who said He was the One of whom David wrote. He said, "I am the good shepherd. The good shepherd gives His life for the sheep" (John 10:11). Our shepherd is *protective*. This is the very nature of a shepherd. He is there to protect his sheep. Without him the sheep could not

find their way to water and life's necessities. The shepherd keeps a constant vigil for wild animals or other dangers that could harm his sheep. Who can forget the story Jesus told of the shepherd in Luke 15 who left the fold to search out the one lost sheep until he found it and carried it back rejoicing all the way?

And there is a final thought. If you have ever witnessed a shepherd at work, he is always in front of the flock. He, unlike a cattle rancher, is not found in the back of his stock driving and whipping them. A shepherd leads the flock. Jesus will never force you to follow. He will never drive you. But, like a shepherd, He is leading you—even now. His sheep hear His voice . . . they know Him . . . and they follow Him. And what a promise: "They shall never perish; neither shall anyone snatch them out of My hand."

A PROMISE AND A PRAYER

"'Rejoice with me, for I have found my sheep which was lost!' I say to you that likewise there will be more joy in heaven over one sinner who repents than over ninety-nine just persons who need no repentance."

LUKE 15:6–7

Lord, You are my Shepherd and I know Your voice. Speak to me today through Your Word as You quicken it to my heart through Your Spirit . . . and I will obey. In Jesus' name, amen.

5 THE PROMISE OF FORGIVENESS

*If we confess our sins, He is faithful and just to forgive us
our sins and to cleanse us from all unrighteousness.*

—1 JOHN 1:9

This is one of the most prominent promises in the Word of God that contains the big "if." God gives His word of honor that *if* we do a certain thing, *then* He will respond in a certain way. In this case, *if* we "confess our sins," *then* He will "forgive us our sins." Forgiveness doesn't just happen. It is preceded by true confession. The man writing down this promise from God was the same John who found his place in the Lord's inner circle along with his brother James and Simon Peter. He is the same John who leaned on the Lord's breast in the upper room. He is the same faithful follower who, when all the others had forsaken the Lord and fled, was standing by Mary's side at the foot of the cross. He was there. He witnessed it all. He heard Jesus say through dry, parched lips as spikes were being driven through His hands and feet, "Father, forgive them, for they do not know what they do" (Luke 23:34).

In John's letter, recorded for all posterity in our New Testament, he used the word *know* thirty times in five short chapters. He drove home the reality that we can know for

certain that our sins can be forgiven and that we can have assurance of eternal life. Near the end of his letter, John affirmed, "These things I have written to you who believe in the name of the Son of God, that you may know that you have eternal life" (1 John 5:13). This personal promise of forgiveness rests on a condition and results in a consequence.

FORGIVENESS OF SINS RESTS ON A CONDITION

Many of God's promises to us are conditional on certain requirements being met by us first. The forgiveness John talked about hinges on a little two-letter, one-syllable word—*if*. "If we confess

> Some believers live without joy in life because days turn into weeks without any true confession of sins.

our sins . . ." Forgiveness is conditional upon the confession of our sins. Some believers live without joy in life because days turn into weeks, and weeks turn into months without any true confession of sins.

The word *confession* is a compound word in Koine Greek, the language of the New Testament. It comes from the combination of a verb meaning "to say" and a word meaning "the same." Literally, *confession* means "to say the same" as God says about our sin. It means that we come into agreement with God about our sin. Sin is not some little vice that we can laugh off as no big deal. It is not something we can

minimize by saying it is not as bad as a lot of other people's sins we know about. It is not something we can simply excuse by pointing out that everyone else is doing it. Your sin—my sin—is so serious that it alone necessitated the cross. The tinge of guilt we often feel in the aftermath of committing sin is in essence the voice of God saying to our hearts, "You have sinned." Confession is our way of "agreeing with God" and responding, "I agree with you, Lord; I have sinned."

We are well adept at having all sorts of ways of avoiding personal responsibility for our own sins. We say, "Oh, that is not worry, it is simply concern." Or, "That is not anger, it is righteous indignation." We say, "That is not lust, simply an appreciative glance." But confession does not say those things. Confession agrees with God about our sin. What we may try and camouflage as concern, God calls the sin of worry. What we like to call righteous indignation, God, who knows our hearts, calls the sin of anger. What we like to think is just an admiring glance, God calls the sin of lust and even says, "Whoever looks at a woman to lust for her has already committed adultery with her in his heart" (Matthew 5:28). Confession gets open and honest in agreement with God, and without it there is no forgiveness of our sins.

> Confession gets open and honest in agreement with God, and without it there is no forgiveness of our sins.

Anyone who has raised children has witnessed an occasion of a spilled glass of milk at the breakfast table. Think about it. The glass is knocked over. Mom or Dad yells, "What happened?" Everyone scrambles to stand up and starts mopping up the milk with their napkins—except, that is, the culprit who knocked it over, who sheepishly responds, "Yeah, what happened?" And so here we are in real life. We cheat on a business deal and God asks, "What happened?" We reply, "It was just the pressure of the economy." Someone enters into an illicit affair and God asks, "What happened?" We reply, "Well, things were not good at home and it was one of those inevitable outcomes that just happen." But confession says, "I knocked over the glass. . . . I cheated someone else. . . . I perpetrated the sin of lust. . . . I am to blame, no one else. . . . I take responsibility. . . . I have sinned." Confession agrees with God on the matter. It does not say, "If I have sinned . . ." The good news is Jesus died on the cross bearing our sins in His own body and taking the punishment for them that we deserved. Forgiveness is free to all—but it is conditional: "*If we confess our sins . . .*"

TRUE CONFESSION ALWAYS RESULTS IN A CONSEQUENCE

If we confess, He will forgive! John was driving home to our hearts one of the real secrets of maintaining fellowship

with Christ, that is, the forgiveness of sins. The word translated *forgive* in our English Bibles finds its origin in a Greek word meaning "to send away." The same word is used when describing the scapegoat that was sent away into the wilderness by the high priest, never to return, symbolically taking with it the sins of the people of Israel. We find this word in the gospels describing how a fever left a certain woman after she felt the touch of Jesus. It is God's desire to send your sins away from you "as far as the east is from the west" and remember them no more (Psalm 103:12).

And by the way, when you confess—and when God forgives—never call unclean again what He has cleansed. Before you move on, know that that tinge in your heart just may be the voice of God saying, "You have sinned." Agree with Him. "If you confess . . . He will forgive."

A PROMISE AND A PRAYER

He who covers his sins will not prosper, but whoever
confesses and forsakes them will have mercy.
PROVERBS 28:13

Lord, my heart is open to You. Convict me of my sin. I agree with You about it; forgive me and cleanse me of all unrighteousness for Jesus' sake and in His name. Amen.

6 THE PROMISE OF THE HOLY SPIRIT

"I will pray the Father, and He will give you another Helper,
that He may abide with you forever—the Spirit of truth."
—JOHN 14:16–17

One of the most instructive and powerful promises to ever escape the lips of our Lord came on the evening before He was crucified, while gathered with His followers in the upper room. Looking into the faces of those men who had left everything to follow Him, who had sailed the rough waters of the Galilee with Him, who had walked the dusty roads of Judea by His side—those very ones who had witnessed people who could not see receive sight, those who could not use their legs walk again, and the dead rise from their tombs—He said, "I am leaving you, but, I am leaving you with this promise. I am going to send another One to come alongside you who will never leave you and who will be with you forever." Then, so as to leave no doubt, He identified this Someone as "the Spirit of truth." This amazing promise made on Mount Zion was kept a few days later on Mount Moriah when the Holy Spirit came on the believers at Pentecost to indwell them—and us—with the promise to never leave or forsake us along the way.

Who really is this Spirit of truth, the Holy Spirit? One of the beautiful attributes of having the New Testament first written in the Greek language is the ability to find hidden gems in certain words that break the code and unlock the deeper meanings of the promises of the Bible. The Greek language is so expressive that certain words and phrases can often be lost in our limited English vernacular. This is never truer than in one simple word found in the promise of this chapter. It is the word *another*. Jesus' promise was that "another" One was coming. The Holy Spirit's true identity is all wrapped up in this little word. There are two different and distinct words used in the Bible to translate into our English word *another*.

Over one hundred times in the New Testament we find the Greek word *heteros*, translated as "another." It means another of a different kind. We get our word *heterosexual* from this word, meaning that a human being can be a male and another human being can be of a different kind, a female. I got my first automobile when I was a teenager. It was a 1956 Chevrolet Bel Air. (I wish I still had it, for it would be worth much more today than the $250 I paid for it then!) Later, I got "another" car. It was a 1967 Ford Mustang. Had I been telling you this story in Greek, I would have used the word *heteros* in describing this. It was another car alright, but one of a different kind altogether.

The other Greek word we translate *another* in our Bible is *allos*. It means another of the exact same kind—same make, same model, same color, same engine, same exact everything. It appears over 150 times in the New Testament. If I took you to the auto dealership in 1967 and showed you another Mustang just like mine—same model, same color, same package, same exact everything—I would use this word to describe to you another car like mine. This is the word that John chose when, in his gospel, he recorded Jesus' promise of the coming of "another" helper, comforter, who would not only abide in us but do so forever. Jesus was letting us know that the Holy Spirit is the same make and model as Himself. In other words, he was saying plainly, "I am coming back to you in the power and in the person of the Holy Spirit. I will help you, lead you, guide you, teach you, comfort you, and fill you with power. And what is more, I will take up residency 'in you' and never leave you again." The Holy Spirit is the same make and model as Jesus.

> The Holy Spirit is the same make and model as Jesus.

For Jesus this was not just a promise made, it was a promise kept. A few days later, on the day of Pentecost, just as He promised, the Holy Spirit came on the believers, indwelling them with power. When you put your faith and trust in

Christ alone and His finished work on the cross to save you, the Father sends His Holy Spirit to come and take up residency in you. This reality is all wrapped up in the mystery of the Trinity. We don't worship three different Gods, only One who manifests Himself in three persons. As the ancient Jewish Shema, repeated in every synagogue every Shabbat, states, "Hear, O Israel: The LORD our God, the LORD is one!" (Deuteronomy 6:4). He is the great three in one. God showed up in all three persons at the baptism of Jesus. The Lord Jesus stood in the Jordan, the Father's voice spoke words of blessing from heaven, and the Spirit descended like a dove. The Father is the *source* of all things. The Son is the *course* of all things, for through Him, and Him alone, the work of salvation was accomplished. And the Spirit? He is the *force* behind it all. He inspired the Bible writers, He convicts us of our sin, He draws us to Christ, and He fills us with power to live the Christian life.

As you turn the page from this chapter, be still for just a moment before the Lord. Meditate on this incredible promise come true. "I will pray the Father, and He will give you another Helper, that He may abide with you forever—the Spirit of truth." He kept His word!

A PROMISE AND A PRAYER

"I will not leave you orphans; I will come to you."
JOHN 14:18

Lord, what You promised You provided. Father, thank You that You see a sparrow when it falls and care much more for me. Jesus, thank You for dying my death so I can live Your life. Holy Spirit, thank You for keeping Your promise, for coming to live *in me*! In Jesus' name, amen.

7 THE PROMISE OF VICTORY OVER TEMPTATION

No temptation has overtaken you except such as is common to man; but God is faithful, who will not allow you to be tempted beyond what you are able, but with the temptation will also make the way of escape, that you may be able to bear it.

—1 CORINTHIANS 10:13

I was seventeen years old, just a few months from high school graduation and the launch from the family nest into the world of university life. I had never heard a prayer in my home, never saw the Bible opened or read in my home, and could count on one hand how many times I remembered being in a church service. After a basketball game one night, a young man shared the good news of Christ with me and witnessed of how his life had been radically transformed by trusting in Christ. I was a bit taken aback, but I must admit I could not remove myself from the power of his testimony. The next Sunday morning he took me to his church where I heard the gospel for the first time, embraced it, and had a life-transforming encounter with Christ. It was months before I remember even hearing the word *repentance*, but I know I repented that day because I immediately began loving what I used to hate and hating what I used to love! Places I liked to go to just the Friday night before, I had zero interest in going to again. And things I never thought I would like to do, such as devouring the Bible and finding fellowship with other believers, I found my greatest joy in doing.

> I know I repented that day because I immediately began loving what I used to hate and hating what I used to love!

As soon as school was over the very next day, I climbed in my car and drove downtown to where I had seen a Christian bookstore. I bought my first Bible that day and discovered the value of Scripture memory. The first verse I ever memorized was not John 3:16; it was 1 Corinthians 10:13 with its promise that God would help me to overcome the temptations that would come my way as a new believer. I deposited this verse in the memory bank of my mind that very day. Because I had hidden it in my heart, only God has recorded how many times across these years when I arrived at temptation's corner, 1 Corinthians 10:13 surfaced in my mind, made a way for me to escape, and kept me from potential mistakes.

It is not a sin to be tempted. Temptation is a reality. It comes our way daily in all sorts of forms and sizes. Your mind is like a hotel. The manager cannot keep someone from entering the lobby. However, he or she can certainly keep that person from getting a room. In a similar way, it is not a sin when some temptation passes through your mind. After all, Jesus was in all points "tempted as are we, yet without sin" (Hebrews 4:15). The sin takes root when we give that thought a room in our mind and let it dwell and get comfortable there. Quite the contrary to the old adage that "The devil made me do it!"—he never made us do anything. He simply dangles his bait in front of us. Then, we are tempted, "drawn away by [our] own desires and enticed" (James 1:14) by that which is outside the boundaries laid out clearly for us in God's Word.

Temptation is *unavoidable*. "No temptation has overtaken you except such as is common to man." Make no mistake about it: as long as we are encased in this human flesh, we will be tempted to sin. It is unavoidable. Think about it. We never have to teach our children to disobey. They pick right up on that due to their nature. We have to teach them to obey. The same is true with God the Father and His children, you and me. Some of us live with the false concept that the longer we walk the Christian pathway and the deeper we go in devotion to God the less we will be tempted. Untrue. Most of our great heroes in the Bible faced their greatest temptations near the end of their pilgrimages, not at the beginning. This

> Do not be surprised when you are tempted. It is unavoidable.

was certainly true of Moses, Elijah, and David. Do not be surprised when you are tempted. It is unavoidable.

But the good news is that God is *unchangeable*. Paul reminded the Corinthians, and us, that "God is faithful." Life may have its shadows, but one thing is rock-solid certain—they are never caused by God's turning or His changing. He is faithful to us. James reminded us that "every good gift and every perfect gift is from above, and comes down from the Father of lights, with whom there is no variation or shadow of turning" (James 1:17).

Not only is God unchangeable in His faithfulness to you, but He "will not allow you to be tempted beyond what you are able, but with the temptation will also make the way of escape, that you may be able to bear it." God provides a way of escape for us. The word picture here is of a mountain pass. Imagine you are surrounded by the enemy as they close in on you from all sides. Then, suddenly, you see an escape route through a narrow mountain pass. You run to it, and through it, to safety on the other side. Most who fall into sin do so willfully because they refuse to take the path of escape that God puts before them.

When temptation comes knocking on our door, we should not let it take us by surprise. It is "common to man." Just because temptation is *unavoidable* does not mean that

the Lord Jesus is not *unchangeable*. Christ Himself is our way of escape. Run to Him. He is forever faithful.

———— A PROMISE AND A PRAYER ————

Blessed is the man who endures temptation; for when
he has been approved, he will receive the crown of life
which the Lord has promised to those who love Him.
JAMES 1:12

Lord, when temptation comes knocking on my door today, as it surely will, cause me to see the way of escape You will provide for me. And give me the grace to run to You. In Jesus' name, amen.

8 THE PROMISE OF VICTORY IN DEATH

Yea, though I walk through the valley of the shadow
of death, I will fear no evil; for You are with me;
Your rod and Your staff, they comfort me.

—PSALM 23:4

*T*here are a lot of voices and volumes around today telling us how to live. Self-help books and motivational videos are a dime a dozen in our world. But there is only one book that tells us how to die. And there is no one verse in this Book of all books that is more poignant and pertinent to the subject than the fourth verse of the most famous of all the chapters of the Bible, Psalm 23, the Shepherd's Psalm.

Tradition holds that King David penned these words about "the valley of the shadow" while sitting in the Judean wilderness between Jerusalem and Jericho. This spot is known today as Wadi Kelt. It is a long valley, four and a half miles in length, and its canyons are as much as fifteen hundred feet deep in some spots. As David sat atop this vast expanse, he saw a spectacular site as he took pen in hand and wrote the twenty-third Psalm. To this day you can sit at this spot as the sun casts a shadow over the canyon on the sheep trails winding their way up and down and across the rugged

terrain. It was there David wrote, "Though I walk through the valley of the shadow of death, I will fear no evil; for You are with me." This one sentence speaks volumes of God's promise to us of our sure victory in death.

An amazing thing happens as we journey verse by verse through Psalm 23. The first part of the psalm is packed with third-person pronouns: "*He* makes me to lie down in green pastures. . . . *He* leads me beside still waters. . . . *He* restores my soul. . . . *He* leads me in paths of righteousness." But then something very up close and personal happens when he begins speaking about death. The pronouns in the psalm change to second person, indicating God's closeness to us in the "valley of the shadow." David now says, "*You* are with me. . . . *Your* rod. . . . *Your* staff. . . . *You* prepare a table for me. . . . *You* anoint my head with oil." As a pastor I have witnessed this on many occasions at the deathbed of believers. The Lord draws very near to them as they cling to His promise, "*You* are with me." Death has its own way of making Christ more personal and near.

> Death has its own way of making Christ more personal and near.

People deal with their own mortality in many different ways. Some *flee* it. They go to the extreme of cryonics, freezing their bodies in hopes that future medical breakthroughs can bring them back to life at some later date. Others *forget* it. They simply reject the idea all together, assuming it will somehow go away if they simply never think about it. Then there are those who *fear* it. They live lives paralyzed with no hope or security in Christ. But there are others, like David, who *face* it. Realizing their days are already numbered in eternity, they have no fear of death because they know the Lord is "with them." David said, "I walk through the valley of the shadow of death." He didn't rush toward it. Nor did he crawl, seeking to postpone it as long as possible. He was not dragged toward it kicking and screaming. He simply walked, comforted by the fact that God was with him and he was not alone.

Death is just a *sojourn*. David indicated that he walked "through" the valley. Death was not his final destination. It was only a brief sojourn, a temporary passage. He knew this path was not a dead end with no way out. It was not a cul-de-sac that got him nowhere. The believer does not walk "in" the valley and stay there. We who have placed our trust in Christ walk "through" the valley. It is just a short and temporary passage from this life into eternal life.

> The believer does not walk "in" the valley and stay there. We who have placed our trust in Christ walk "through" the valley.

There is tremendous comfort in this passage knowing that death is simply a *shadow*. In Proverbs 30:5, David's

son, King Solomon, reminded us that "every word of God is pure." Note carefully that David said this is the valley of the "shadow" of death. No believer ever walks through the valley of death, simply the "valley of the shadow of death." The Lord Jesus is the One who walked through the valley of death for us—for three days and three nights. Then He emerged alive again from the empty tomb exclaiming, "Behold . . . I have the keys of Hades and of Death" (Revelation 1:18).

Thus, the believer only walks through the valley of the "shadow" of death. A shadow might frighten you, but it cannot harm you. As you approach the front door of your home at night and are about to place the key in the door, the porch light might cast a shadow that causes you to step back a moment in fear, but nothing about it can harm you. And the only way a shadow can be cast is if there is a great light shining. David said he walked "through" the valley of the shadow. That is just what we do with a shadow—we walk right through it.

It is no wonder in the very next verse David said, "I will fear no evil." He knew death was defeated; it was only a temporary passage "through" a shadow into the light. He could "fear no evil" because of the knowledge that the Lord was with him. Jesus has conquered death, hell, and the grave (Revelation 1:18). It is no wonder we, too, fear no evil. We have a precious promise when we arrive at our own

appointment with death. We can join David in the confident assurance that "You are with me!"

Because Jesus said, "I am He who lives, and was dead, and behold, I am alive forevermore" (Revelation 1:18), those of us who are believers need not fear death. We are only headed "through" the valley of the shadow of death, and Jesus is with us every single step of the way. There is victory not just over death but in death as well.

—— **A PROMISE AND A PRAYER** ——

For this is God, our God forever and ever;
He will be our guide even to death.
PSALM 48:14

Lord, what comfort to know that I do not have to fear death. It has "lost its sting." And thank You for the promise that when that time comes for me, You will never leave me. In Jesus' name, amen.

9 THE PROMISE OF RESURRECTION

*"I am the resurrection and the life. He who believes
in Me, though he may die, he shall live. And whoever
lives and believes in Me shall never die."*

—JOHN 11:25–26

*I*t was a sad and somber day in the little village of
Bethany on the eastern slope of the Mount of Olives as
Jesus stood beside a brokenhearted family at the grave of their
brother, Lazarus. Looking into their sorrowful faces He made
one of the most astounding promises in all the Bible: "I am
the resurrection and the life. He who believes in Me, though
he may die, he shall live. And whoever lives and believes in Me
shall never die." Then, to prepare His disciples for His own
resurrection, He called Lazarus forth from the grave. The
resurrection of Christ is what separates Him from a thousand
other gurus and self-proclaimed prophets who have appeared
time and again across the centuries. And it is His resurrection
that assures our own in that coming great day.

JESUS' DEITY

This promise includes a word about His *deity*. By using the
words "I am" when he stated, "I am the resurrection and

the life," He was capturing the attention of all those around as to His real nature and true identity. John's gospel records one of these "I am" statements by Jesus on seven different occasions. We first hear of this expression of the name of God way back in Exodus on the backside of a desert when Moses asked the voice emerging from a burning bush to identify himself. God spoke again and instructed Moses to go back and tell the captive children of Israel in Egypt that "I AM has sent me to you" (Exodus 3:14). When Jesus said, "I am," all those within the sound of His voice recognized this as an affirmation of His deity, that He was not a mere man; He was God Himself, clothed in a garment of human flesh.

The most fundamental element of the Christian faith is that Jesus was not just some astute teacher or "another one of the prophets"; He was God incarnate. It was at this very point that the apostle Paul said, "He is the image of the invisible God . . . all things were created through Him and for Him" (Colossians 1:15–16). It was this deep assurance and steadfast holding to this promise that would later lead Paul—and most all the disciples—to a martyr's death. They all insisted, "Jesus is Lord!"

> The most fundamental element of the Christian faith is that Jesus was not just some astute teacher or "another one of the prophets"; He was God incarnate.

THE REALITY OF DEATH

This precious promise also includes a word about *death*. His promise was, even though we would one day die, it would not be the end; we would "live again." Many of us live in complete denial of our coming appointment with death. One of the surest facts of life is that you are going to die. One day your heart will beat for its last time and you will inhale and exhale your last breath. Recently I was looking through some old family photo albums, and I came to a startling revelation. In those earlier pictures my hair was a lot darker and my face was obviously a lot less wrinkled. It dawned on me that this body of mine has death in it. I am decaying, and it is happening right before my eyes. In denial of this fact, some people opt for plastic surgery or liposuction, or they fill themselves with vitamin-enriched foods and various supplements. But none of that can stop the fact that we are marching toward our own divine appointment of meeting our Maker.

Death is the common denominator of all men. In the morning, when you read the newspaper, on the society page you will read about only one class of people. In the sports section you will read about those gifted in the athletic arena. In the business section those who are highly successful are highlighted. But turn to the obituary page and there you find everyone listed side by side in cold alphabetical order. Death comes knocking on the door of the billionaire and the poorest of the poor, lists them side by side in the obituary column, and sends them both out to stand before the Judge of all the universe.

OUR DESTINY

Finally, this promise contains a word about our *destiny*. "Though he may die, he shall live." The body may die but there is a part of us, our spirit, that will live on as long as God lives. There is another life more than a million times longer than this one. A hundred years from today you will be alive . . . someplace. For the believer, Jesus promised, "Whoever lives and believes in Me shall never die."

> There is another life more than a million times longer than this one.

At the conclusion of this eternal promise, the Lord paused, looked squarely into their faces, and asked a question. In fact, it is life's bottom-line question, "Do you believe this?" Do you believe this promise about deity, death, and destiny? I often wonder how this would have sounded if we had a video as this encounter played out that day at Lazarus's tomb. Or if we just had an audio recording. I look at this question and wonder where Jesus put His inflection. Did He ask, "Do *you* believe this?" After all, the question is intensely personal. Or perhaps He asked, "Do you *believe* this?" It

is a very pointed question as well and is centered in where our faith and trust are placed. His interest is not in whether we give intellectual assent to His claims, but do we really believe this, have we placed our faith in Him and in Him alone? Perhaps He asked the question in this manner: "Do you believe *this*?" That is, this promise of victory over death.

You are the only one who can answer this bottom-line question of life because it is intensely personal, it is pointed, and it is so precise. As for me, thankfully, I addressed this question long ago by placing my trust in Christ and declaring, "Yes, Lord, I believe that You are the Christ, the Son of the living God!" How about you? Do you believe this?

—— A PROMISE AND A PRAYER ——

For it pleased the Father that in Him all the fullness should dwell, and by Him to reconcile all things to Himself, by Him, whether things on earth or things in heaven, having made peace through the blood of His cross.
COLOSSIANS 1:19–20

Lord, I believe that You and You alone are my resurrection and my life. Thank You for the promise that my faith in You assures that I shall never die. In Jesus' name, amen.

10 THE PROMISE OF SALVATION

Believe on the Lord Jesus Christ, and you will be saved.

—ACTS 16:31

*I*t is okay to ask questions. In fact, there are more than 150 questions recorded in the gospels that came from the lips of our Lord Himself. And these are only the ones that were recorded and found their way into the sacred writ. Jesus was always asking questions. It did not matter whether He was in a one-on-one conversation, in a small circle of people, or in the midst of a gathering crowd, He probed the hearts of His hearers by asking questions. He was not asking questions because He was seeking answers. He is not only omnipotent (all powerful), but He is omniscient (all knowing). He knows everything about everyone—their actions, their omissions, even their thoughts. Never once do we come upon Him in the Bible exclaiming, "Wow, that was a surprise. I didn't see that coming!" Never. He is all-knowing. He asked questions not for answers but in order for us to see for ourselves, to think for ourselves, in order to come into a "knowledge of the truth."

People often approached Him with questions of their own. Once, Nicodemus, a learned member of the Jewish supreme court, came to Jesus in the evening hours and was

told by the Lord that he needed to be born again. Not understanding Christ was referring to a spiritual birth, he asked, "How can a man be born when he is old? Can he enter a second time into his mother's womb?" (John 3:4).

Christ was once sought out by a lawyer with the intent of testing Him with what he perceived to be a hard question. He asked, "Teacher, which it the greatest commandment in the law?" (Matthew 22:36). Jesus replied by saying that we should love the Lord God with all our being and that a second commandment was like it, to love others as we love ourselves.

After the resurrection and upon hearing Him speak of the coming of the Holy Spirit, the disciples asked, "Lord, will You at this time restore the kingdom to Israel?" (Acts 1:6). And who can forget the question of the apostle Paul on the Damascus road: "Lord, what do You want me to do?" (Acts 9:6).

But, the most pointed question ever asked in the Bible is the question asked by a jailer in the city of Philippi, which immediately preceded the promise of salvation of this chapter. Having witnessed a great earthquake that shook the very foundations of the prison and opened all its doors, he fell at Paul and Silas's feet, asking, "What must I do to be saved?" (Acts 16:30). And there you have it. This is the question that should be asked by every person who has ever lived. It is pointed, penetrating, personal, and extremely pertinent. Without batting an eye or thinking for even a moment, they answered him—and us—by saying, "Believe on the Lord Jesus Christ, and you will be saved" (Acts 16:31). What is it we must do to be saved? In a word, *believe*!

> What is it we must do to be saved? In a word, *believe*!

This promise of salvation is found in the context of Paul and Silas's incarceration. The jailor, after having beaten their backs with a whip until they were striped with deep lacerations, securely locked them in the inner depths of the prison. At midnight he heard the two prisoners singing songs of praise at the top of their lungs. Then, suddenly, the place was shaken by a great earthquake, which resulted in the prison doors flying off their hinges. Knowing his own fate would be death if the prisoners escaped his care, he was about to fall on his own sword when he realized that Paul and Silas were still there, although they could have easily fled. He fell on his knees in conviction before them, asking, "What must I do to be saved?" (Acts 16:30).

The jailor wondered what he had to *do* to be saved. But the truth is, he could not *do* anything to be saved. It had already been done. Christ's death on the cross is what saves. Many today fall into this same trap. It seems so logical in our performance-driven culture. Some seem to think salvation

is spelled *d-o* when, all the while, it has been spelled *d-o-n-e*. It is available for any and all of us through the finished work of Christ on the cross.

The apostle wasted no time in pointing out the answer—"Believe!" That is it—"Believe on the Lord Jesus Christ, and you will be saved." This faith to believe is built on fact—the fact of the death, burial, and resurrection of Christ. Note carefully, the instruction was to believe "on" the Lord. Prepositions in Greek are powerful and expressive. Paul did not use the preposition we translate "in" (*en*). Nor did he use the Greek preposition *eis*, which describes "into," that is, a movement toward something that had not necessarily reached its destination. He used a preposition in Greek (*epi*) that means "upon." The promise is for those who believe "on," who lay their trust on, the Lord Jesus. I may believe in George Washington, but I don't believe on him. I do not trust my life to him. And the word *believe* is recorded here in the aorist tense, meaning it is punctiliar—at a set moment of time he believed, he transferred his trust to Christ alone to save him. Salvation is not something we grow into. It is a crisis moment, experienced in a moment of time when we believe on the Lord and transfer our trust from ourselves to Him alone for our salvation.

A beautiful encounter ensues before this story ends: this redeemed jailer "took them the same hour of the night and washed their stripes" (Acts 16:33). Just hours earlier he had lashed their backs until they were bloody; now he gently washed the wounds he had put there. Only the gospel can instantaneously change our hearts like this. You and I have a precious promise, the promise of salvation. "Believe on the Lord Jesus Christ, and *you* will be saved." Claim it . . . right now.

—— A PROMISE AND A PRAYER ——

If anyone is in Christ, he is a new creation; old things have passed away; behold, all things have become new.
2 CORINTHIANS 5:17

Lord, thank You for the reminder that there is nothing I can do to earn or merit Your favor. Through Your work on the cross and victory over the grave it has already been done for me. I believe *on* You. In Jesus' name, amen.

11 THE PROMISE OF HIS ABIDING PRESENCE

"Go therefore and make disciples of all the nations, baptizing them in the name of the Father and of the Son and of the Holy Spirit, teaching them to observe all things that I have commanded you; and lo, I am with you always, even to the end of the age."

—MATTHEW 28:19–20

*W*hat an experience it must have been for those early believers as they gathered on the Mount of Olives and witnessed Jesus ascending back into heaven before their very eyes. As He left, what would be His parting words to them and to us? He left us with a promise: "I am with you always." There are almost nine thousand recorded promises in the Bible, but this is the one that He wanted us to hold especially close to our hearts. It is one thing to know that He is *for* us, our advocate with the Father, but it is something altogether more assuring to know that He is *with* us always, no matter who we are, where we are, or what we have done.

This is the one promise that is woven like a thread throughout the entire Bible, showing up time and again throughout the Scriptures, all the way to the very last verse of the last chapter of the last book, Revelation. When Moses heard God's call to return from the desert to become the

great emancipator of His people, God spoke this promise from a burning bush saying, "I will certainly be with you. And this *shall be* a sign to you that I have sent you: When you have brought the people out of Egypt, you shall serve God on this mountain" (Exodus 3:12). Then after leading the people through the Red Sea into the wilderness wanderings for forty years, Moses' final words to the people before he died and they entered the promised land were in the form of a reminder: "He is the One who goes before you. He will be with you, He will not leave you nor forsake you; do not fear nor be dismayed" (Deuteronomy 31:8). Joshua held to this promise as he led the people into their promised possession.

During the time of the Judges, Gideon was faced with the seemingly insurmountable odds of facing the great Midianite army with just a handful of men. Just when he needed a word from God, the Lord spoke to him saying, "Surely I will be with you, and you shall defeat the Midianites as one man" (Judges 6:16). He was and he did! Then, in the days of the kings, when things looked bleak for King Jehoshaphat as he faced a threatening coalition of Ammonites and Moabites, the prophet spoke saying, "Do not fear or be dismayed; tomorrow go out against them, for the LORD is with you" (2 Chronicles 20:17).

We could go through the Bible seeing this same promise appearing over and over. David said, "I will fear no evil."

Why? "For You are with me" (Psalm 23:4). In a moment of great need, God promised Isaiah, "When you pass through the waters, I will be with you" (Isaiah 43:2). Jeremiah was comforted when faced with the Babylonian invasion with these words from the Lord: "Do not be afraid of the king of Babylon . . . for I am with you" (Jeremiah 42:11). Then, after their return from exile, the prophet Haggai spoke God's message to them, "I am with you, says the LORD" (Haggai 1:13). During the days of revival under good King Josiah, Zephaniah brought words of hope to the people from the Lord: "The LORD your God [is] in your midst" (Zephaniah 3:17).

In the New Testament, we find the promise of Christ's abiding presence with us laced throughout its pages. In the upper room, Jesus told the disciples that He would "pray the Father, and He will give you another Helper, that He may abide with you forever" (John 14:16). Jesus ascended back to heaven with this promise: "I am with you always" (Matthew 28:20). And the final verse in the Bible leaves us with this promise of Christ's presence through His grace: "The grace of our Lord Jesus Christ be with you all" (Revelation 22:21). There

> There is no promise in the entire Bible repeated so many times, to so many different people, in so many different circumstances, as this one: "I am with you always."

is no promise in the entire Bible repeated so many times, to so many different people, in so many different circumstances, as this one: "I am with you always."

We see this truth beautifully illustrated in the parable Jesus told about a man who had two sons. The younger son took his inheritance, ran away for the bright lights of the big city, and wasted everything. Later, in remorse and repentance, he returned home to a welcoming and forgiving father who held a big party for him. But when the band was playing, and people were feasting and rejoicing, the father noted someone was missing from the festivities. The older brother was "angry and would not go in" (Luke 15:28). Wallowing in his own self-pity, he bemoaned the fact that he was a faithful son and their father had never thrown a big party for him in such a fashion. The Father pulled him aside with these assuring words, "Son, you are always with me, and all that I have is yours. It was right that we should make merry and be glad, for your brother was dead and is alive again, and was lost and is found" (Luke 15:31–32). This father in the story is a picture of your heavenly Father who has a reminder for you this very moment: "You are always with me, and all that I have is yours." The story ends rather abruptly without our ever knowing how the older boy responded. Perhaps so that you can complete the story today by resting in Jesus' promise, "I am with you always."

Promises made are appreciated. But, as I said before, promises kept are what mean the most. Jesus promised, "I am with you always." Believe it. Hold to this promise. And when, like Jeremiah, you pass through the waters, remember: He is with you—always!

A PROMISE AND A PRAYER

"Fear not, for I am with you; be not dismayed, for I am your God. I will strengthen you, yes, I will help you, I will uphold you with My righteous right hand."

ISAIAH 41:10

Lord, no matter where I may go today—no matter how high I may climb, or how low I may fall—I believe and hold to Your promise that You are with me now and always. In Jesus' name, amen.

12 THE PROMISE OF GOD'S ABIDING WORD

*The grass withers, the flower fades, but the
word of our God stands forever.*

—ISAIAH 40:8

This past spring my wife, Susie, planted a beautiful array of colorful spring flowers. It was not long before they withered and faded away as the months gave in to the hot Texas heat. As I watched their demise, this verse from Isaiah came to my mind with its promise that God's Word will never fade away but will stand as long as God lives.

Most of the books of centuries past are lost in the darkness of antiquity. But the Bible is different from any other book ever written. It is actually a library in itself of sixty-six different books written over a period of more than fourteen hundred years by at least forty different authors. Some were callus-handed fishermen, others were kings, prophets, doctors, shepherds, and rabbis. Yet the Bible has one theology, one plan of redemption, and one theme woven through its pages, leaving no explanation for its unique and lasting nature other than the fact that behind the pen of each writer was the hand of God Himself.

THE PROMISE HAS A SUPERNATURAL ORIGIN

We can rest in the Bible's promise of its abiding forever due to its *supernatural origin*. Writing to young Timothy in his last pastoral letter before his own execution, Paul said that "all Scripture is given by inspiration of God" (2 Timothy 3:16). The Scripture you hold in your hands and read each day has been "given" to you. Unlike all other books, it is supernatural in its origin. It originates with God, not with man. The phrase "given by inspiration" means "God-breathed." God used men in the process of giving us His Word. But He did not breathe on them. He breathed out of them His abiding Word. Just as a skilled musical composer creates a score utilizing flutes and trumpets, strings and percussion as his instruments, so God chose His own instruments, some as different as common laborers and powerful kings, and breathed out His words through them. Your Bible is "given" to you by God Himself.

> Your Bible is "given" to you by God Himself.

Simon Peter threw light on how this happened when he declared that "holy men of God spoke as they were moved by the Holy Spirit" (2 Peter 1:21). The identical Greek word translated here as "moved" was used by Luke in describing Paul's shipwreck in the book of Acts. There came a fierce

storm, and the sailors on board the ship lost all control, unable to guide the ship because of the strong winds. They stayed busy about their tasks, but the winds took the ship wherever it blew (see Acts 27:15–17). Just as the sailors on board the ship were active yet had to relinquish control over where it would go, so it was with the Bible writers. In a very real sense, the writings were not their own. God Himself made this point clear to His prophet Jeremiah saying, "I have put My words in your mouth" (Jeremiah 1:9).

And, as Paul wrote to Timothy, this includes "all" Scripture (2 Timothy 3:16). That little three-letter, one-syllable word is extremely inclusive. King Solomon framed it such: "Every word of God is pure" (Proverbs 30:5). Earlier his father, King David, said, "The law of the LORD is perfect" (Psalm 19:7). Though we might find more worth in reading the Sermon on the Mount in Matthew 5 than we find in reading the long list of unpronounceable names in the genealogy found in Matthew 1, each word of each verse in the entire book is equally inspired. We can rest in God's promise that the Bible will abide forever because of its *supernatural origin*. All Scripture, every word of every verse of every chapter, is God breathed, inspired by Him. Since, unlike all other books, the Bible originates with God and not with man, it "stands forever."

THE PROMISE HAS A SUSTAINING OUTCOME

We can rest in this promise not only due to its *supernatural origin* but also because of its *sustaining outcome*. It "is profitable for doctrine, for reproof, for correction, for instruction in righteousness, that the man of God may be complete, thoroughly equipped for every good work" (2 Timothy 3:16–17). It is the Word of God that sustains the believer along the journey of the Christian life. We begin this journey with "doctrine," proper teaching that shows God's plan of salvation and sanctification. What if we veer off the path? It becomes profitable for "reproof" of our sin. But He doesn't leave us there in defeat and despair; the Bible is profitable for "correction." It provides us a restart. Finally, it sustains us by being profitable to us for "instruction in righteousness."

Paul recognized the wisdom of this sustaining outcome. He wrote Romans to emphasize the importance of doctrine. He wrote the Corinthian letters to show the need of reproof. Galatians flowed from his prolific pen to emphasize the need of correction. And in Ephesians he highlighted instruction in righteousness.

Yes, we can trust in the promise of God's abiding Word to us that stands forever because of its *supernatural origin* and its *sustaining outcome*.

On a cold winter afternoon in 2002, we buried my ministry father, W. A. Criswell. As he had requested, as the casket

closed on his lifeless body, there lying open on his chest was a copy of the Bible, God's holy Word. It was opened to his favorite verse for all to see: "The grass withers, the flower fades, but the word of our God stands forever" (Isaiah 40:8).

Dr. Criswell often closed a message on the Bible with the story of Sir Walter Scott. As the great Scottish poet lay dying on his deathbed, he turned to his son-in-law, Lockhart, and said, "Son, bring me the book." Lockhart replied, "Father, what book? There are thousands of books in your library. What book?" "Oh," the great wordsmith replied, "there is just one book. Bring me the book." Lockhart went to the library and picked up the Bible, brought it back, and laid it in the hands of Sir Walter Scott. And the great man died with the Bible clutched within his hands.

Yes, there is just one book! And we can have and hold to this abiding promise: "The grass withers, the flower fades, but the word of our God stands forever" (Isaiah 40:8).

A PROMISE AND A PRAYER

For prophecy never came by the will of man, but holy men of God spoke as they were moved by the Holy Spirit.

2 PETER 1:21

Lord, thank You for this precious treasure, Your holy Word, Your own personal love letter to me. Open my eyes to see Your truth and quicken these—Your own words—to my heart at the very point of my need. In Jesus' name, amen.

13

THE PROMISE OF
ANSWERED PRAYER

*"Ask, and it will be given to you; seek, and you will
find; knock, and it will be opened to you."*

—MATTHEW 7:7

This is one of the most amazing promises in all the
Bible. Jesus calls us to simply ask, and then He makes a
startling promise that when we do, He will give it to us. And
yet who of us has not asked something near and dear to our
hearts and waited and waited without ever getting that thing
or that one for which or for whom we asked. Looking back
over my own life, I have come to the place where I am thank-
ful God did not give me some of the things for which I asked
Him. During my college years I dated a wonderful Christian
girl. As a new believer, the Lord brought her into my life at
just the right time to encourage me in the faith. Then came a
day, after two years in a relationship, that she broke up with
me and fell in love with another young man. I was crushed.
During the next many months, I asked the Lord every night
to bring her back to me. He used those days to strip away
all my pride, to drive me to Himself, and out of it I clearly
heard His voice calling me into the gospel ministry. Then, a
few months later, I met the girl who stole my heart, the very

one God had planned for me to spend my life and ministry with in the first place. And today, more than fifty years later, she has been all I could ever have hoped for in a wife and life partner.

THE WILL OF GOD

The particular promise of answered prayer can only be understood when we find it wrapped securely in the will of God. Our highest aim in life should be to bring glory to God (1 Corinthians 10:31), and this includes making sure our prayers are prayed in accordance to His will. Some pray in a presumptuous attempt to alter God's will. But this is impossible. God said, "I am the LORD, I do not change" (Malachi 3:6). Take your cue from the Lord Jesus as He agonized in prayer in Gethsemane's garden hours before facing the cross: "Not My will, but Yours, be done" (Luke 22:42). Effective prayer is always wrapped up in praying according to God's will. The apostle John reminded us, "This is the confidence that we have in Him, that if we ask anything *according to His will*, He hears us. And if we know that He hears us, whatever we ask, we know that we have the petitions that we have asked of Him" (1 John 5:14–15, emphasis added). We can ask anything, if it is

> Our highest aim in life should be to bring glory to God.
>
> 1 CORINTHIANS 10:31

according to His will, and then we can rest in the confidence that we can *know* He will answer us.

This promise, "Ask and it will be given you," is made to those of us who know God's will in the matter for which we are praying. If we are certain of His will, then He invites us to "ask" with the promise that we will receive from Him that for which we have asked. This is why when one prays and places their trust in Christ, they can be confident that it is the Lord's will that none should "perish" and thus have the confidence that they can ask and receive. God has made it plain that He is "not willing that any should perish but that all should come to repentance" (2 Peter 3:9). Therefore, when we know the will of God in the matter, we do not have to seek or knock, but we simply ask, and He answers.

> When we know the will of God in the matter, we do not have to seek or knock, but we simply ask, and He answers.

SEEK AND YOU WILL FIND

But what about those matters on our hearts for which we are praying but we are uncertain as to the will of God in the matter? This brings us to the next level of prayer in our promise of answered prayer. You are to "seek and you will find." When you don't know His will, seek it until you find it. This is a deeper and more mature level of prayer because it puts self aside and is motivated by a deep desire to want to know the will of God in a matter. It involves an intense search for the heart of God coupled with a regular pattern of Bible reading. This is why the apostle Paul admonished us to "let the word of Christ dwell in you richly in all wisdom" (Colossians 3:16). We most often find God's will through His Word.

We are to keep on seeking with an intensity that goes far beyond our simply asking and receiving. The promise is that we will "find" God's will for our lives if we keep seeking and do not give up. He does not want to veil His will from us. In fact, He is more interested in our finding His will for our lives than we are ourselves.

KEEP ON KNOCKING

Finally, what about those times when we are certain we know God's will in the matter for which we are praying but the answer has not yet come? Jesus said it was in those times that we should "knock." The verb tense tells us to keep on knocking with the promise that the door of answered prayer will be opened to us. This requires tremendous perseverance.

There is a sense in which God deals with His children in the way we deal with our own. When they are toddlers, we teach them to "ask" for certain things. Later, we teach them to "seek" after their desires. We don't do all their math

homework for them. We teach them to seek the answers themselves. And the time comes, when they are older, when because we know what is best, we teach them to "knock" with real earnestness until doors are opened for them.

When you pray, remember that answered prayer is always centered in God's will. He knows what is best for us. So, there are times we simply ask. There are other times that demand our seeking. And there are other times when we keep on knocking and never give up. And we have His precious promise: "It will be given to you . . . you will find . . . it will be opened to you."

A PROMISE AND A PRAYER

This is the confidence that we have in Him, that if we ask anything according to His will, He hears us.
1 JOHN 5:14

Lord, my highest aim is to bring You glory. The best way I can do so is to know and do Your will for my life. Teach me, Lord, to do Your will and to know what it is to join Jesus in praying, "Not my will, but Yours, be done." In Jesus' name, amen.

14 THE PROMISE OF POWER

"You shall receive power when the Holy Spirit has come upon you; and you shall be witnesses to Me in Jerusalem, and in all Judea and Samaria, and to the end of the earth."

—ACTS 1:8

When the time came for Christ to leave earth and return to heaven after a sojourn of thirty-three years, He left us with a challenge to witness of His love not only at home but to the "end of the earth." A few days earlier, on a mountain in Galilee, He had left us with what we call the Great Commission: "All authority has been given to Me in heaven and on earth. Go therefore and make disciples of all the nations, baptizing them in the name of the Father and of the Son and of the Holy Spirit, teaching them to observe all things that I have commanded you; and lo, I am with you always, even to the end of the age" (Matthew 28:18–20). Knowing our own frailties, He knew this gigantic task—not just to reach a few locals but entire nations—could not be accomplished in our own strength. We would need a power outside our own. Thus, He left us with a promise that we would "receive power" when the Holy Spirit came upon us.

THE "WHO" QUESTION

In order to know and appropriate this promise of power from on high demands the answer to several questions. First, there is a *who* question. Jesus left us with these words, "*You* shall receive power." This promise of power for the express purpose of being His "witnesses" to a lost world is one Jesus has given to each and every one of us. That includes *you*. Earlier in Acts 1 the disciples were enamored as to when He would return and restore the kingdom. The Lord let them know it was not for them "to know times or seasons" (Acts 1:7).

Jesus was plain. We are not to be His chart makers or date keepers but His "witnesses"—all of us . . . you and me! None of us are exempt from this basic element of Christian living—that is, to share the good news of Christ.

> We are not to be His chart makers or date keepers but His "witnesses."

THE "WHAT" QUESTION

You shall receive what? Power! This is the great need of believers today. We all need supernatural power to live the Christian life. We have seen already that there are two words that describe the difference in the first-century believers and many today: influence and power. Today we pride ourselves on influence, who we know and how we can influence the

culture. But these early believers to whom Christ was speaking did not have enough influence to keep Peter out of prison. They were virtually void of influence with any of the civil or religious authorities. But the more important news was that they had the power to pray him out!

When Jesus promised us "power" He used a word from which we derive our English word *dynamite*. It results in an explosive type of boldness in the life of the believer. The entire book of Acts is the story of a group of common men and women—just like you and me—who, despite all the bigotry and bias of a Roman-ruled world, went out in power from a little upper room in Jerusalem to tell the story of a publicly executed Jew. How did they do this in the face of such persecution and opposition? They had a new power, a dynamite nature, that had come upon them and brought with it a new dynamic. They believed His promise: "You shall receive power."

THE "WHEN" QUESTION

When did they receive this power? When the Holy Spirit came upon them. There should be no such thing as a Christian without power. When you receive Christ, you have the Holy Spirit. He comes to take up residency in you. Thus, you have this power now. When Susie and I married, we had a new Chevrolet. Well, to be honest it was not exactly new,

but it was new to us. One morning I got in the car and turned the key. Silence. Nothing. Upon raising the hood, I discovered that during the night someone had stolen the battery, rendering that beautiful, shiny car useless without a battery to get it started and energize it. I thought about that car as I have been typing this chapter. Many of us get all dressed up and ready to go in the Christian life but never seem to get started. Why? We need a power outside of us to energize us. We have a promise, the promise of power. But it comes only as we yield our lives to the Holy Spirit.

> Many of us get all dressed up and ready to go in the Christian life but never seem to get started.

THE "WHY" QUESTION

Why does God promise us power when the Holy Spirit comes upon us? "To be His witnesses." There should be no such thing as a Christian who is not a witness. If you have Christ, you have the Holy Spirit. If you have the Holy Spirit, you have power. And if you have this power, you will be His witness as you journey day by day in the normal traffic patterns of your life.

The Lord never called you to be a judge, sitting in condemnation of others. He did not call you to be a prosecuting attorney, pointing your finger of accusation at others. He did not call you to be the defense attorney, seeking loopholes to

help others get past the law. He did not call you to be on the jury, weighing evidence against someone else. He called you to simply be a witness, to tell others of what you have seen and heard.

God entrusted this holy gospel to such common people, void of formal training, but they received power and became His witnesses to the end of the earth. Think of this awesome power that resides in each of us who have placed our faith and trust in Christ alone. Promises given must become promises claimed and appropriated. God has given you a promise of power: "You shall receive power when the Holy Spirit has come upon you; and you shall be witnesses to Me." Confess it . . . and claim it!

———— A PROMISE AND A PRAYER ————

"The Holy Spirit will come upon you, and the
power of the Highest will overshadow you."
LUKE 1:35

Lord, thank You that I have in You all I need to live my life today with power. Live Your life through me today as, by faith, I appropriate this power to boldly share Your name. In Jesus' name, amen.

15 THE PROMISE OF HIS LISTENING EAR

*Now this is the confidence that we have in Him, that if
we ask anything according to His will, He hears us. And
if we know that He hears us, whatever we ask, we know
that we have the petitions that we have asked of Him.*

—1 JOHN 5:14–15

When taken at face value, this is one of the most remarkable prayer promises in all the Bible. God is saying that we can know with certainty that He will not only hear us but grant our prayer petitions when we ask Him to do so. However, it comes with a caveat. We have the assurance of answered prayer only when we ask "according to His will." Even as I type these words, I wonder how much we really believe this. Here is a promise from God that can change not only us but everything around us, if and when we believe it and apply it to our lives.

ELEMENT 1: WE ASK

There are three important elements involved in this promise: We ask . . . He hears . . . we know. First, *we ask*. This promise begins with a qualifier, "*If* . . . we ask." There is a big "if" inserted here for good reason. The reason some of us never

have our prayers answered is that we never actually ask Him for anything. Asking is not that hard. If you can say, "Pass the gravy," you can pray. James got right to this point when he said, "You do not have because you do not ask" (James 4:2). Many of us wonder why we live outside the blessing and provision of God, and the answer is, we simply never ask Him for anything. We wonder why our kids get into trouble until we realize that we never asked Him to keep them pure. Our marriages are teetering on disaster and we come to the realization that we never asked God to help us and keep us together, which is His will for us. We sometimes struggle to make ends meet until we realize that asking God for help has usually been a last resort instead of a first. God is waiting on many of us to simply ask Him to bless us.

> God is waiting on many of us to simply ask Him to bless us.

But this promise is not an "anything for the asking" proposition. Read it all: "If we ask anything . . . according to His will." This is the whole crux of the matter when it comes to answered prayer. That is, lining up with God's will in our petitionary pleas. The place to begin finding God's will is in God's Word. He will never lead you to pray for anything that runs contrary to what He has firmly set out in His Word. His will is made known through His Word and by His Spirit to us. "The Spirit also helps in our weaknesses. For we do not know what we should pray for as we ought . . . He makes intercession for the saints according to the will of God" (Romans 8:26–27). When we are not certain of God's will in a matter, the Holy Spirit will take God's Word and pray for us "according to the will of God." This promise is given to us to encourage us to ask great things from Him.

ELEMENT 2: GOD HEARS

We ask. And, when we do, *He hears.* "If we ask anything according to His will, He hears us." We have a God who hears us when we pray. Think of that. In the Old Testament God invited His people to "call upon Me and go and pray to Me, and I will listen to you" (Jeremiah 29:12). The psalmist of Israel rested in this truth saying, "Certainly God has heard me; He has attended to the voice of my prayer" (Psalm 66:19). In the New Testament, Simon Peter professed that "the eyes of the LORD are on the righteous, and His ears are open to their prayers" (1 Peter 3:12).

Not only does God hear us, but He joins us in prayer, making intercession for us (Romans 8:27) before His Father's throne. If I believed the Lord Jesus heard my prayers, and if I could hear Him taking my requests and praying for me right now in the next room, I would

> If I could hear Him taking my requests and praying for me right now in the next room, I would not fear a million foes.

75

not fear a million foes. And yet the reality is that He is hearing, and He is praying for me right now. We ask. He hears.

ELEMENT 3: WE KNOW

When we ask and He hears, then *we know.* As our Bible promise states, "If we know that He hears us, whatever we ask, we know that we have the petitions that we have asked of Him." We don't have to hope we have that for which we have asked. We do not have to wish for what we have asked. We don't have to think or assume we will have that for which we have asked. We can have the assurance of knowing that what God has promised, He will perform.

Most of us live out what we genuinely believe about prayer. If we seldom pray, it is because we really do not think He can do much. If we pray without faith, it is because we really do not trust Him, no matter how much we may try to convince ourselves and others that we do. What kind of fellowship would you have with your husband or wife if you had no confidence at all that what they had promised you would be fulfilled? You cannot trust someone until you really know them. When we know Christ in the intimacy of Father and child, we will trust Him and believe that what He promises to us He always provides. No wonder John said, "This is the confidence that we have in Him!"

We ask. . . . Go ahead; it is not that hard. *He hears*; His

ears are open to our prayers. And when we ask and He hears, *we know* "we have the petitions we have asked of Him." We can trust Him. What He has promised, He will provide.

—————— A PROMISE AND A PRAYER ——————

For the eyes of the L<small>ORD</small> run to and fro throughout the whole earth, to show Himself strong on behalf of those whose heart is loyal to Him.

2 C<small>HRONICLES</small> 16:9

Lord, thank You that even now as I offer up this brief prayer You are hearing me. While others may look on the outward appearance, You are looking at my heart. Thank You for the confidence that You really answer prayer. In Jesus' name, amen.

16 THE PROMISE OF PARDON

Seek the LORD while He may be found, call upon Him while
He is near. Let the wicked forsake his way, and the unrighteous
man his thoughts; let him return to the LORD, and He will have
mercy on him, and to our God, for He will abundantly pardon.
—ISAIAH 55:6–7

*A*t the end of each United States presidential term the
president issues pardons to certain men and women
who are incarcerated or who have been convicted of various
crimes. Governors of the various states also have this power
vested within their state offices. A pardon exempts someone
from punishment for a crime they have committed. It rests
solely on an executive decision and is not subject to any judi-
cial review. The Creator of the universe has broad pardon
powers, but pardons are not granted to everyone. They are
available to those of us who "seek" Him, "call" to Him, and
"return" to Him.

Our God does not simply promise to pardon us but to
"abundantly" pardon. He goes above and beyond a pardon
to "justify" those whom He pardons. The Bible says, those
"whom He called, these He also justified" (Romans 8:30).
This is something altogether different from a pardon and is
wrapped up in the thought of His promise to not only pardon

us but to do so abundantly. No court of law can justify someone for their offense. A court may acquit someone, or even pardon someone, but it cannot "justify" someone. They cannot make the particular offense as if it never happened. But God can—and God does. He abundantly pardons and does not simply exempt us from punishment but wipes our slate clean as if it had never happened and we had never sinned. This is why the Bible says Jesus will one day present us "faultless before the presence of His glory with exceeding joy" (Jude v. 24).

> Our God does not simply promise to pardon us, but to "abundantly" pardon.

This promise of a heavenly pardon comes to us with a cause and effect attached. Not everyone will be pardoned of their sin. This promise is for those who meet three criteria listed in the context of God's promise to "abundantly pardon." The pardon is given to those who "seek" the Lord, who "call" on Him, and who "return" to Him.

PARDONS ARE FOR THOSE WHO SEEK THE LORD

Don't be confused at this point—a pardon does not come in seeking it, but in seeking the Lord. All through Scripture we are called to seek Him. Perhaps you need power to overcome something that has entered your life. It does not come in

seeking power but in seeking Him: "I sought the LORD, and He heard me, and delivered me from all my fears" (Psalm 34:4). Perhaps you are financially challenged and in need of monetary help. Don't seek it. Seek the Lord, who said of Uzziah, "As long as he sought the LORD, God made him prosper" (2 Chronicles 26:5). Are you looking for happiness and contentment? You may be looking in all the wrong places. The Bible promises that those who seek the Lord will rejoice and be glad (Psalm 70:4). It might be that wisdom is your need of the day. "Those who seek the LORD understand all" (Proverbs 28:5). The wisest people I have known are not those with degrees from esteemed institutions of higher learning but those whose lives are characterized by their seeking the Lord continually.

> Are you looking for happiness and contentment? You may be looking in all the wrong places.

The Bible admonishes us to seek Him "while He may be found." This brings the element of urgency into the equation. There is not always going to be adequate time to call on Him. We derive our word *callous* from the Greek word found in Ephesians 4:19 where Paul described someone who is "past feeling." I have a callus on the bottom of my foot. I can stick a pin in it and not feel it. There comes a time when after one repeatedly rejects Christ that His heart "hardens" toward spiritual things like a callus and he becomes "past feeling."

It is not that the Lord ceases to call but that we can reach a point where we cease to hear and feel. Seek the Lord while He may be found. There will not always be adequate time.

PARDONS ARE FOR THOSE WHO CALL ON THE LORD

Next, if you are in need of pardon, "Call upon Him while He is near." Perhaps even as you read these words you sense His nearness to you in this moment. Call on Him. No one has ever sought and found the Lord without calling out to Him. He promised, "Call to Me, and I will answer you, and show you great and mighty things, which you do not know" (Jeremiah 33:3). I cannot think of anything simpler than to call on Him. Those who have never prayed can call to Him from their hearts. He is "able to do exceedingly abundantly above all that we ask or think" (Ephesians 3:20).

PARDONS ARE FOR THOSE WHO RETURN TO THE LORD

And finally, pardons come to those who "return to the Lord." This thought is best pictured in the story of the prodigal son who "returned" to his father, seeking him and calling to him, and received his father's full pardon and restoration. Isn't it time for us to "forsake" our wrong ways and thoughts and simply return to Him? Here is repentance—a change of

mind, which affects a change of volition or will, which causes a change of action. We seek Him. We call on Him. We return to Him.

God promises, "You will seek Me and find Me, when you search for Me with all your heart" (Jeremiah 29:13). And here is the good news. Before you ever decided to seek Him, He took the initiative and sought you. Jesus said He came to "seek and to save that which was lost" (Luke 19:10). That is the Lord Jesus knocking on your heart's door now. Seek Him while He may be found. Call on Him while He is near. Return to Him. And when you do, "He will have mercy . . . He will abundantly pardon."

A PROMISE AND A PRAYER

"I will forgive their iniquity, and their sin I will remember no more."
JEREMIAH 31:34

Lord, before I ever thought of seeking You, You came to me, knocking on my heart's door, pulling at my heart's strings, calling me to Yourself. I call out to You today, while You are so near. Thank You for the promise that You have "abundantly pardoned" me. In Jesus' name, amen.

17   THE PROMISE OF JOY

Sing praise to the Lord, you saints of His, and give thanks
at the remembrance of His holy name. For His anger
is but for a moment, His favor is for life; weeping may
endure for a night, but joy comes in the morning.

—PSALM 30:4-5

A few years ago our culture was saturated with what we
called "Good News-Bad News" jokes. For example,
the doctor tells the patient there is good news and bad news.
"The good news is you have forty-eight hours to live and get
your house in order. But the bad news is I have been trying
to call you for two days." We had our share of these jokes
circulating through the church as well. There is the one
about the pastor who stood before the congregation with the
good news that the church had enough money to not only
pay off the church debt but to build the new building debt-
free as well. When the applause and the amens subsided, he
gave them the bad news. "The bad news is it is still in your
pockets!"

There is good news and bad news in God's promise to
us recorded in Psalm 30:5. The bad news is that "weeping
may endure for a night." But the good news is the promise
that "joy comes in the morning." For those who are in the

83

> For those who are in the darkness of the night where weeping endures, there is help and hope just around the corner.

darkness of the night where weeping endures, there is help and hope just around the corner. Joy is coming in the morning.

TEARS OF DISCOMFORT

The *bad news* is weeping endures for the night. There are many kinds of tears that flow from our eyes. There are tears of *discomfort*. These tears flow out of our hearts and eyes during times of bereavement. Most of us have been there and know the tears of separation Mary and Martha of Bethany felt with the death of a loved one. There are tears of *disappointment*. These tears flow when we lose our job, don't get the house we wanted, don't make the team, or fail to get the part in the school play.

TEARS OF DEFEAT

Some tears flow during times of *defeat*. We see it in one form or another as we watch the Olympic games. Peter met great personal defeat when he denied our Lord and then went out and "wept bitterly" (Matthew 26:75).

Then there are altogether different tears like those of *devotion*. They flow when we are so much in love we cannot help but express ourselves. On one occasion a woman

washed Jesus' feet with her tears of love and devotion (Luke 7:36–38).

TEARS OF DESPERATION

Often the tears we shed are tears of *desperation*. I have seen these tears flow in all kinds of circumstances: when kids were seriously sick or when a spouse has deserted. Once in the gospels Jesus was confronted with a man whose child was sick, and he said with tears, "Lord, I believe; help my unbelief" (Mark 9:24).

TEARS OF DELIGHT

There are also tears of *delight.* We get the good report from the doctor, or we sit rejoicing at a wedding, and like Joseph and his brothers being reunited, we can't hold back tears of delight.

Weeping endures through the night. But you can cry your eyes out with all the types of tears mentioned above, and when all is said and done none of that worldly sorrow can bring about life, much less the kind of joy that comes in the morning. This promise of joy in the morning does not simply mean that we can get everything all cried out during the nighttime hours and when we wake up in the morning everything will be fixed. No, of course it doesn't. There is only a certain type of your tears that brings the promise of

joy in the morning. This is the point of Paul's words to the Corinthians, and to us: "For godly sorrow produces repentance leading to salvation, not to be regretted; but the sorrow of the world produces death" (2 Corinthians 7:10). The only kind of weeping that brings real joy is godly sorrow that leads to repentance. When we weep over our own sin we will understand the truth of this promise.

THEN, THE GOOD NEWS

The *good news* is "joy comes in the morning." The one who truly knows what it is to be so burdened by their sinful state without Christ is the one who can know true and lasting joy—in the morning. Why? Because the tears of true godly sorrow lead to repentance. When we begin to weep over our own sin and get right with God, joy is on the way. When we weep over this in the night, we have the promise of joy in the morning. The world tells us in the words of the old Broadway song to "pack up your troubles in an old kit-bag

> When we begin to weep over our own sin and get right with God, joy is on the way.

and smile, smile, smile." But it never works. Everything we try to cover, God has a way of uncovering. And everything we uncover before Him in godly sorrow and repentance, He covers over with His blood, and a shout of joy then follows in the morning.

There is a spiritual paradox in play with this promise. In our quest for joy some of us have learned to put on a happy face, smile, and fake it. But real joy never comes because we do not know real sorrow. We know a variety of different types of tears, but the tears shed in godly sorrow over our own sin are often missing. Since some of us know only superficial sorrow, we only experience superficial joy. Real joy is the product of genuine sorrow over sin. Weeping may endure for the night—and sometimes the nights can be awfully long. But we have and hold to a promise from God that is as sure as the sun rises in the morning: "Weeping may endure for a night *but . . .* joy comes in the morning!"

A PROMISE AND A PRAYER

Though now you do not see Him, yet believing, you rejoice with joy inexpressible and full of glory, receiving the end of your faith—the salvation of your souls.

1 PETER 1:8–9

Lord, thank You for the promise that no matter how dark my night may be—no matter how helpless and hopeless things may appear—Your joy, full of glory, is on the way and coming "in the morning." In Jesus' name, amen.

18 THE PROMISE OF AUTHENTIC DISCIPLESHIP

"Follow Me, and I will make you become fishers of men."

—MARK 1:17

*P*erhaps no other subject is talked about more and practiced less in Christian circles than authentic discipleship. Discipleship is in the very heart of the Great Commission our Lord gave to the church when He instructed us to "Go therefore and make disciples of all the nations" (Matthew 28:19). The church is commissioned to "make disciples," not just add to its numbers, stand for justice, or meet the social needs of its community. Authentic disciples are "made." They don't just happen into being.

> The church is commissioned to "make disciples," not just add to its numbers, stand for justice, or meet the social needs of its community.

JESUS CALLS US TO HIMSELF

When we turn just one page in our Bibles from the Great Commission into Mark's gospel, we discover what authentic discipleship is really about. The first word Jesus ever used to describe who would become followers of Him was not *Christian*. In fact, this word didn't come into being until years later when Barnabas and Paul went to Antioch and "taught a great many people. And the disciples were first called Christians in Antioch" (Acts 11:26). Nor was the first word to describe believers *disciples*. We do not encounter this word until Matthew 10. The first term ever to escape Jesus' own lips to describe what He desired His followers to be was "fishers of men" (Mark 1:17). In Jesus' mind authentic discipleship always involves two actions: following and fishing.

Authentic discipleship is found in following Christ. He said to Simon Peter and his brother, Andrew, "Follow Me." Follow Me—those two simple words were used so often by Jesus. Not only on the Sea of Galilee—where He encountered a group of fishermen engrossed in their lifetime passion of the fishing business and saw them put down their nets to begin the journey of following Him —but also around the coast of the lake at Capernaum. There He saw a Jew taking up tax money from the local Jewish residents for the Roman government. Jesus looked squarely into his face and spoke those two words, "Follow Me." Matthew threw down his money pouch, walked away from his tax office—his livelihood—and took his first steps to becoming an authentic disciple. Authentic disciples are men and women who truly follow Christ wherever He leads them.

JESUS ENABLES US WITH HIS POWER

Jesus followed up those two words with "I will make you become" authentic disciples. When the Lord says He will "make" us into disciples, He uses a word in Greek that describes a work of art. He forms us like a potter with his clay. He frames us like an artist with her canvas. And, like a poet with his pen, He fashions us into a unique creation. When we follow Christ, He causes us to become interested in what He is interested in. And what is that? It is why He came in the first place: "to seek and to save that which was lost" (Luke 19:10). First, He calls us to Himself ("Follow Me") and then He enables us with His power ("I will make you") to become authentic disciples.

> When we follow Christ, He causes us to become interested in what He is interested in.

FISHING FOR FOLLOWERS

Authentic discipleship is found not only in *following* but in *fishing*. What does He make us to become when we begin following Him? Fishers of men! Therefore, if we are not "fishing" we are not "following"—if we, like the twelve, have begun following, the natural result will be that we are fishing for men. That is, we have a burning and unquenchable desire to share the good news, resulting in seeing people come to personal faith in Christ.

Years ago I heard an analogy from a forgotten source that opened my own eyes to authentic discipleship. Suppose those of us called to be fishers of men started planting fishing clubs all over the world. In every city these men and women gathered in their local clubs and week by week, month by month, they talked about their love for fishing. They even charted the growing numbers of fish to be caught in the lakes all around them. They soon developed strategies aimed at how they would go about catching these fish and even came up with several catchy slogans that they used in all their publications. Very subtly they became so busy in their clubs that they ceased fishing.

They organized themselves into state fishing conventions and even local associations and were constantly searching for new and better ways to fish. Some of the brightest among them became authorities and even wrote books on fishing, though they had never personally caught a fish themselves. They began publishing houses, and soon their local clubs were filled with materials on how and where to fish. They gathered in large conventions to motivate their numbers in the art of fishing. They hired staff and formed numerous committees in their local clubs. But neither the staff nor the committee members ever wet a hook themselves.

Then they began to build bigger and better headquarters for their national leaders as well as large buildings for their

local gatherings. They even started schools to teach fishing courses. But the teachers never fished. They just taught about it. So every year graduates would be given fishing licenses. They returned to help teach in the local clubs . . . but never fished.

Some of these local fishermen lived on the banks of the lakes and ponds and could smell the stench of the dead fish floating on the lake. But they never actually fished. Can you imagine how distressed they were when someone finally suggested that if they were not fishing, they were not really fishermen, no matter how many times they attended the local clubs or how eloquently and passionately they could speak about fishing? Which brings us to a question: Is a person a fisherman if year after year he or she never catches a fish? Or, more personal and more pertinent: Is a person a true follower of Christ if year after year he never shares Christ with those around him?

> Is a person a true follower of Christ if year after year he never shares Christ with those around him?

Jesus gave us a promise: "Follow me and I will make you become fishers of men." According to Jesus, if we are not fishing, we are not following—no matter how much we may know or how perfect our attendance may be at our local fishing club each Sunday.

This promise was first given to Simon Peter. He did something about it. He left his nets and followed. Three and a half years later, this crusty, callus-handed fisherman stood on the Temple Mount, preached the gospel, and cast his net into the crowd, and three thousand people came to faith in Christ that day. Can you hear the Lord Jesus saying to you across these centuries, "Follow Me"? And here is the promise, "I will make you to become fishers of men."

A PROMISE AND A PRAYER

Those who sow in tears shall reap in joy . . .
bringing his sheaves with him.
PSALM 126:5–6

Lord, someone I know needs to know You today. Help me—make me—to become a fisher of men and speak with boldness the goodness of salvation to all who believe. In Jesus' name, amen.

19   THE PROMISE OF GREATER WORKS

"Do you not believe that I am in the Father, and the Father in Me? The words that I speak to you I do not speak on My own authority; but the Father who dwells in Me does the works. Believe Me that I am in the Father and the Father in Me, or else believe Me for the sake of the works themselves. Most assuredly, I say to you, he who believes in Me, the works that I do he will do also; and greater works than these he will do, because I go to My Father. And whatever you ask in My name, that I will do, that the Father may be glorified in the Son."

—JOHN 14:10–13

With this powerful promise, Jesus invited us on an adventure into the realm of God's unlimited possibilities. With the caveat of our belief in Him, He promised that we will *equal* His own works: "The works that I do he will do also." But there is much more to this promise. The Lord goes on to say we will not simply equal His works but *exceed* them—"Greater works than these he will do."

This is one Bible promise that should stop us dead in our tracks. It is one thing to be able to equal the Lord's works, but how can we begin to exceed them? After all, He left a legacy of some amazing deeds. The church has a mindset that "the only hands that God has are my hands" and "He helps those who help themselves." Consequently, we come to a promise such as this, and our first inclination is to roll up our sleeves and work as hard as we can on all kinds of plans and programs to further the work of Christ—and we fall short every single time.

ACCEPT A PROMISE

The key to understanding this promise is found in the last phrase of the text. Jesus said we would have the capacity to equal and exceed His works "because I go to the Father." What does this mean? What happened when He went back to heaven? He explained it four verses later in John 14 when, after informing His followers that He was leaving them, He said, "And, I will pray the Father, and He will give you another Helper, that He may abide with you forever—the Spirit of truth" (John 14:16–17). Again, the key to understanding is in the word *another*, which here means another of the same make and same model as Jesus! Jesus was leaving, but He was coming back in the form of His Spirit to live in the lives of every believer. Instead of just one carpenter walking around Galilee, now there would be hundreds, and then millions,

> Instead of just one carpenter walking around Galilee, now there would be hundreds, and then millions.

spread all over the world with Christ alive in them equally and exceeding the works He did in that thirty-three years.

Jesus has two bodies. When He invaded planet Earth, He had an earthly body in which He lived, and in that earthly body was a heavenly authority. After delivering the Sermon on the Mount, the people were "astonished at His teaching, for He taught them as one having authority, and not as the scribes" (Matthew 7:28–29). Jesus made it plain from whence came His authority when He said, "The words that I speak to you I do not speak on My own authority; but the Father who dwells in Me does the works" (John 14:10). Jesus declared that the same authority that resided in His physical body resides in His spiritual body: the church—you and me!

We cannot stop reading this promise too soon. After promising greater works on our part and telling us He was going back to the Father, He added the connecting word— *And*. "And whatever you ask in My name, that I will do, that the Father may be glorified in the Son." Prayer is not what brings about the greater work—prayer *is* the greater work. This is why, before every great undertaking, every marvelous miracle, we find Jesus pausing to pray to the Father, tapping into the true source of authority and power. When the disciples returned frustrated at their failure to see God work in their own behalf, Jesus pinpointed their problem: "This kind does not go out except by prayer and fasting" (Matthew

17:21). Like the early believers' failures, most all our failures are prayer failures.

APPLY A PRINCIPLE

So what is the key to "greater works" for us? The first step is to *accept a promise*. Jesus said "whatever" we ask He will do. Next, we must *apply a principle*. The promise of answered prayer is based on praying in Jesus' name. He said, "Whatever you ask in My name. . . ." This is not some little catchy formula, or a tag line assigned to the end of our prayers. When we lay our petitions down before the Father in the throne room of prayer, we come to God on behalf of all Jesus is and all He has done. Most of us have come to the end of a busy day when nothing went right, feeling guilty and unworthy, and we prayed something like, "Lord, I know I don't have any right to ask You for anything tonight." Then God says, "Suppose things had been different. Say you had begun your day early at 5:00 A.M. and prayed an hour, led a person to Christ during the day, and done everything right. Would you feel more like praying?" If your answer is yes, then you may be praying in your own name. If you had prayed for five hours and led ten people to Christ, you would have no more right to ask for anything

> God does not grant our requests on the basis of who we are or what we have done but on the basis of who Jesus is and what He has done.

because God does not grant our requests on the basis of who we are or what we have done but on the basis of who Jesus is and what He has done. It is "whatever you ask in My name."

ACTIVATE A POWER

When we accept this promise and apply this principle, we *activate a power*. "I will do [it], that the Father may be gloried in the Son." Jesus did not say, "I will help you do it." He said, "I will do it." And for the express purpose that the Father may be gloried. God will move heaven and earth to answer prayers that give Him glory. Yes, Christ is still alive, in you, in me—and all over the world today "greater works" are being done for His glory.

A PROMISE AND A PRAYER

"And whatever things you ask in prayer, believing, you will receive."
MATTHEW 21:22

Lord, thank You for the realization this very moment that Christ is alive—in me! And that You answer my prayers not on the basis of who I am or what I have done but on the basis of who Jesus is and what He has done. In Jesus' name, amen.

20 THE PROMISE FOR THE CHURCH

"And I also say to you that you are Peter, and on this rock I will build My church, and the gates of Hades shall not prevail against it."
—MATTHEW 16:18

This promise from the lips of our Lord that He will build His church, and nothing—not even the gates of hell — can stand against it, comes on the heels of one of the most misunderstood of all Jesus' claims and statements. Peter had just made the "great confession" that Jesus was indeed "the Christ, the Son of the living God" (Matthew 16:16). Then Jesus looked him squarely in the eyes and said, "You are Peter, and on this rock I will build My church" (v. 18). For centuries the Roman Catholic Church has proclaimed that Christ built His church on Peter, whom He called the "rock." The massive Saint Peter's Basilica stands in the Vatican as a testimony to this interpretation. However, the language of the New Testament suggests something quite different. The neuter noun in Greek suggests that it was Peter's confession that "Jesus is Lord" that was the rock on which Christ would build His church, not Peter himself. And thus, for two millennia, every time someone comes to Christ making a confession of their faith in Him alone, Christ lays another

> Every time someone comes to Christ making a confession of their faith in Him alone, Christ lays another stone into the building of His body, the church.

stone into the building of His body, the church.

WE ARE A PRIVILEGED CHURCH

There are several important factors of note found in Christ's promise, "I will build My church." While we read this promise in our Bible in a linear manner, I have often wondered where He put the inflection in this particular promise. Perhaps He put the emphasis on the first word—"*I* will build My Church" to indicate to us that we are a *privileged church*. He is the One who builds His church. His church is not built by plans, programs, promotions, pastors, or people. The fact that He is the One who is building His church still today all around the world shows how supernatural the church is in its very being and existence. We are privileged that He chose us as living stones to make up His church.

WE ARE A PERMANENT CHURCH

It could be that Christ emphasized, "I *will* build My church." After all, we are a *permanent church*. The future tense indicates this is an ongoing process as He continues to build His church across the centuries. The Roman Empire tried

to stamp the church out. But it was the power of the gospel through the church that ultimately defeated the Romans. In our day radical Islam is on the move in massive efforts to eradicate the Christian faith as they martyr believers and destroy church buildings in Syria, Iran, Afghanistan, and on and on. But we have and hold to the promise of our Lord that He "will" continue to build His church around the world until He comes again in great glory.

WE ARE A PROGRESSIVE CHURCH

We are also a *progressive church* in the sense that convert upon convert, stone upon stone, Jesus progresses forward in building His church. He promised, "I will *build* My church." This is why when Peter wrote his own letter in the New Testament, he declared, "Coming to Him as to a living stone, rejected indeed by men, but chosen by God and precious, you also, as living stones, are being built up a spiritual house . . . acceptable to God through Jesus Christ" (1 Peter 2:4–5). Even as you read this book, the Lord Jesus is at work all over the world, building His church living stone by living stone.

WE ARE A PURCHASED CHURCH

It may well be that Jesus' inflection and emphasis was on the next to the last word in this promise, "I will build *My* church." We are a *purchased church*, bought by Christ with the price of His own blood. The church belongs to Him, not us. Something becomes ours when we make full payment for it. Your automobile becomes yours only when the loan is paid off. Until then, it is owned by the bank. But once you have paid for it in full, it truly becomes your car. When Jesus calls the church *"My* church" He is indicating that it came at a price. He did not go to the cross and put down a little down payment; He paid the price in full with His own shed blood. This church of which we are a part is His, not ours.

> The church belongs to Him, not us.

WE ARE A PECULIAR CHURCH

Finally, had we been there at Caesarea Philippi that day, we might have heard, "I will build My *church*." The church is not a high-steeple, stained glass, Greek-columned edifice. The Greek word for church means "the called-out ones." We are a *peculiar church* in the sense that God has called out a people for His own from every tribe, nation, and people. This is why Peter, who made the great confession, later said of the church, "You are a chosen generation, a royal priesthood, a holy nation, His own special people, that you may proclaim the praises of Him who called you out of darkness into His marvelous light" (1 Peter 2:9). Think of it! We are His "own special people," the called-out ones. From generation to generation to generation across this church age, He has been building His church. There is coming a day when the final living stone will be put in place. The building will be completed, and Christ will come again to receive us unto Himself so that where He is we will forever be also. Until then, we have and hold to His precious promise, "I will build My church."

The real issue is whether you have joined Peter in making your own great confession. If not, why not? He is calling you now. Join Peter and the rest of the redeemed. Believe it. Confess it: "You are the Christ, the Son of the living God."

———— A PROMISE AND A PRAYER ————

Now to Him who is able to do exceedingly abundantly
above all that we ask or think, according to the power
that works in us, to Him be glory in the church by Christ
Jesus to all generations, forever and ever. Amen.
EPHESIANS 3:20–21

Lord, You and You alone are the one and only Christ, Anointed One, Messiah, the true Son of the living God. I am overwhelmed that You have placed me, a living stone, in the building of Your church. In Jesus' name, amen.

21 THE PROMISE OF REST

"Come to Me, all you who labor and are heavy laden, and I will give you rest. Take My yoke upon you and learn from Me, for I am gentle and lowly in heart, and you will find rest for your souls."
—MATTHEW 11:28–29

We live today in a restless world where we are moved and motivated by overachievement, long hours, rushing and scampering around until we are depleted of much of our energy and effectiveness. Our busyness is compounded by our desire for immediate gratification. "Give it to me, and give it to me right now" is our command and cry. Our culture has ingrained this into our psyche. If we want popcorn, we don't want to wait for it the old-fashioned way; we pop it in the microwave. The days of the encyclopedias are past as search engines like Google and others place information on any and all subjects at our fingertips in seconds. Many of us are exhausted, drained dry, running on gas fumes, and hanging by a thread.

For such a time as this, Christ offered up a promise: "I will give you rest." Jesus originally spoke these words to a people who were being weighted down by the impossible task of attempting to keep the Jewish laws and the standards the laws imposed. They were at the point of exhaustion. Hard

as they may have tried, they could not measure up. So, in a feeble attempt to alleviate their anxiety, they simply kept trying harder. Does this sound familiar to anyone? Jesus came to them, and to us today, with a proposition to stop trying and start trusting Him, with His accompanying promise that we will find the very thing for which we are searching: "rest for our souls."

HIS PROMISE IS SIMPLE

He began with an invitation. Here is the *simplicity of His promise*: "Come to Me." Jesus did not offer us a twelve-step approach, nor any five pillars of peace through submission, but a simple invitation—"Come to Me." He simply offered us Himself. A little child learning to walk can understand this word, *come*. Christ called us to come not to some plan, program, principle, or procedure, but to a Person. "Come to Me." Note all the personal pronouns in this promise. Seven times in these short verses He referred to Himself—Me, I, My, Me, I, My, My.

How can we find rest for our souls? Come to Jesus. He is the only one who understands because there is nothing about our journey He hasn't already experienced. He confessed that "foxes have holes and birds of the air have nests, but the Son of Man has nowhere to lay His head" (Matthew 8:20). No matter my need, I can come to Jesus. When I am in sorrow,

I can come to the One who was Himself "a Man of sorrows and acquainted with grief" (Isaiah 53:3). His promise to give us rest is a simple one. Anyone can do it. "Come to Me." Come to Jesus.

> How can we find rest for our souls? Come to Jesus.

WE ARE ALL WELCOME

We find not only the simplicity of His promise but the *scope of His promise*. He invited "all who labor and are heavy laden" to come to Him. No one is excluded. The rich and the poor are invited. The well and the sick may come. The old and the young are welcome. The educated and the illiterate are all on the invitation list. Everyone, everywhere, is part of this promise: "Come to Me . . . *all* of you who are in need . . . And I will give you rest." Rest is the gift of God to us. We don't get it through prescriptions or pills. We don't get it through energy and efforts. He gives it freely to *all* who simply come to Him.

THE SERENITY OF REST

But there is more to this promise. Not only is it found in its simplicity and scope but in the *serenity of His promise. Rest.* For many, that is such an elusive word. Jesus' promise to give us "rest" is multifaceted. There is the rest that is found in our salvation, for it is "not by works of righteousness which

we have done, but according to His mercy He saved us" (Titus 3:5). When we come to Jesus in repentance of our sin—believing in His finished work on the cross and His resurrection from the dead—and find new life in Christ, our first conscious awareness is in the peace that comes over us, the load of sin that is lifted from us, and the "rest" that we find in Him. When I had this salvation experience as a seventeen-year-old who could count on one hand how many times he had ever been inside a church building, my first impulse was a peaceful "rest" that I found in coming to Jesus.

This rest involves what Jesus called a rest for our souls. He promised we would find "rest for our souls." He continued, "For My yoke is easy and My burden is light" (Matthew 11:30). The yoke of the law was heavy, unmanageable, burdensome, too much to bear up under. But Jesus frees us from the law, puts us under His grace, and bears our burdens for us. The yoke He offers us is one of grace. Its burden is light. John framed it like this: "For this is the love of God, that

> The yoke He offers us is one of grace.

we keep His commandments. And His commandments are not burdensome" (1 John 5:3). His commandments to us are twofold: Love God . . . love others! (Matthew 22:37–39).

The offer still stands: "Come to Me. Trust in Me with all your heart and lean not to your own understanding . . . and

you will find rest for your souls." It all begins in a simple act of coming to Jesus.

A PROMISE AND A PRAYER

But those who wait on the LORD shall renew their strength;
they shall mount up with wings like eagles, they shall run
and not be weary, they shall walk and not faint.
ISAIAH 40:31

Lord, I am resting in the joy of who You are. I am finding out the greatness of Your loving heart. Jesus, I am resting in You. In Jesus' name, amen.

22 THE PROMISE OF OVERCOMING

Therefore submit to God. Resist the devil and he will flee from you. Draw near to God and He will draw near to you.

—JAMES 4:7–8

We have an enemy. His name is Satan, and the Bible describes him in terms of being a "roaring lion, seeking whom he may devour" (1 Peter 5:8). Ever since he confronted Adam and Eve in the garden with his subtle and subversive ways, he has been about the business of deploying his forces of evil with the goal of the ultimate defeat of every believer. Along the way, we have become quite adept at passing the blame for our own sinful decisions on to him. We have virtually worn out the phrase, "The devil made me do it." We inherited it from our first parents and have pretty much perfected it in our avoidance of taking personal responsibility for our own sin.

We may have a persistent protagonist in the devil, but we also have a precious promise from the Lord. He promises to "draw near" to us and to cause the devil to "flee" from us. James laid out three verbs for us that are all in the imperative mood, signifying they are commands for us and not options from which we may pick and choose. We are to "submit to

God." We are to "resist the devil." And we are to "draw near to God." And when we do, we have His overcoming promise that the devil will take momentary leave from us and God Himself will come very near to enable, energize, and encourage us along our journey of life.

THERE IS A PREREQUISITE

Many well-meaning believers rush into this promise attempting to resist the devil and draw near to God, but they completely ignore the first phrase of the verse, which calls us to "submit to God." Our ability to resist satanic influences and overcome in life has a prerequisite. First and foremost, it calls on us to live a life of submission to God's will and way and not to insist on our own. To *submit* literally means to "line up under." The first step in overcoming our setbacks and sins is to place ourselves under the lordship of Jesus Christ. This is accomplished by a single act of our will, which precludes always having our own way. Our life becomes characterized by "His will, not our will" and "His way, not our way." It is closely akin to the prayer Jesus Himself prayed on the eve of the crucifixion in Gethsemane's garden: "Not My will, but Yours, be done" (Luke 22:42).

> Our ability to resist satanic influences and overcome in life has a prerequisite.

THERE IS A PROPOSAL

James challenged us, once we have submitted to God's will, to oppose evil, to "resist the devil." This Greek verb literally means "to stand against." It is a military phrase ordering us to take a stand against someone or something. This entails the defensive aspect of our struggle against the devil. Paul had this in mind when he wrote from his first Roman incarceration. He was most likely looking at the Roman guard standing over him as he wrote, "Take up the whole armor of God, that you may be able to withstand in the evil day, and having done all, to stand. Stand therefore, having girded your waist with truth, having put on the breastplate of righteousness" (Ephesians 6:13–14).

Many of us live defeated Christian lives because we are fooled by this demonic deceiver. But, for the most part, the devil is not the problem—we are. Consider this promise: "Resist the devil and he will flee from you." Do we really believe this? We would if we realized he is already a defeated foe. John attested to this fact when he acknowledged, "He who is in you is greater than he who is in the world" (1 John 4:4).

Satan's doom is already sealed. When Jesus said, "All authority has been given to Me in heaven and on earth" (Matthew 28:18), it was an indication that if He has "all" authority, then Satan, in actuality, has *none*. The only authority he can exert over you is that which you allow him to have when you fail to "submit to God" and "resist the devil."

> Satan's doom is already sealed.

THERE IS A PROPOSITION

Finally, James concluded with, "Draw near to God and He will draw near to you." The only way we can approach God, much less draw near to Him, is through the blood of His Son and our Savior, the Lord Jesus Christ. This is why Paul said, "In Christ Jesus you who once were far off have been brought near by the blood of Christ" (Ephesians 2:13). Jesus left us a beautiful word picture of this in His parable of the prodigal son. As the rebellious boy submitted in repentance and drew near to home, the father saw him while he was a great way off and ran to meet him along the road. As the boy drew near to the father, the father drew near to him. In the same way, when we submit to Christ's lordship over our lives, making His will our will, when we stand against devil through the blood of Jesus, Satan flees from us as we draw near to God.

James finished this paragraph in the New Testament letter bearing his name with an admonition to each of us, "Humble yourselves in the sight of the Lord, and He will lift you up" (James 4:10). To humble ourselves before God is to admit our spiritually bankrupt condition apart from Christ

and to acknowledge our dependency on Him. How much more satisfying to have Christ exalt us before others than to try our own feeble attempts of self-exaltation? Yes, "God resists the proud, but gives grace to the humble" (James 4:6).

We have this precious promise that the devil will "flee from us" and God will "draw near to us." But like many of His promises, it is conditional. We must "submit to God . . . resist the devil . . . and draw near to God." And when we do, we step into a new dimension of a life of overcoming and victory, experiencing for ourselves what it is when the Creator God of this universe actually draws near to us.

A PROMISE AND A PRAYER

You are of God, little children, and have overcome them, because He who is in you is greater than he who is in the world.
1 JOHN 4:4

Lord, Your will and Your way be done in me today. Thank You that as I draw near to You in submission of my life, I have Your promise to draw near to me at the same time. In Jesus' name, amen.

23 THE PROMISE OF POTENTIAL

The righteous shall flourish like a palm tree.

—PSALM 92:12

*T*rees play a unique part in the biblical narrative. God seems to have a way throughout the Scriptures of positioning us in relation to various trees in order to teach us valuable life lessons and to pronounce some of His most amazing promises to us. For example, we find Adam "behind" a tree, hiding from the very God who created him. Adam sinned, and the Lord came to mend the broken relationship, but Adam "hid . . . from the presence of the LORD God among the trees of the garden" (Genesis 3:8). Later, we find the prophet Elijah "under" a tree. After his thunderous victory over the prophets of Baal on Mount Carmel, he fled in fear from wicked Queen Jezebel, ran all the way from Dan to Beersheba, climbed under a juniper tree in deep depression, and said, "It is enough! Now, LORD, take my life" (1 Kings 19:4). But God met him, strengthened him in the way, and gave him a promise that propelled him to some of his greatest days of ministry and miracles. Remember Zacchaeus? We find him "up" a tree in the city of Jericho. But Jesus spotted him, gave him a promise, and he began a brand-new life.

One of the most descriptive promises in all the Bible is

found in Psalm 92:12. The Lord promised that the righteous person shall flourish and grow "like a palm tree." This promise, seldom known by many, is so fully descriptive of God's faithfulness to those who live righteous lives. To understand and apply this promise calls us to observe three truths. The person described is one who is "righteous." The potential discovered is that this person will "flourish." And the picture detailed reveals that he or she will flourish in the same way as "a palm tree."

THE PERSON DESCRIBED

It is imperative to begin by noting the *person described*. This promise is addressed to that one who is "righteous." But we meet an apparent dilemma. The Bible tells us "there is none righteous." And to add emphasis, the verse continues, "no, not one" (Romans 3:10). The Bible is also clear in saying that "all our righteousnesses are like filthy rags" (Isaiah 64:6). While it is true in and of ourselves that we are unrighteousness, it is also true that in Christ Jesus the Lord is our righteousness (Jeremiah 33:16). When we put our faith in Christ, we can say with Isaiah, "He has clothed me with the garments of salvation, He has covered me with the robe of righteousness" (Isaiah 61:10).

> While it is true in and of ourselves that we are unrighteousness, it is also true that in Christ Jesus the Lord is our righteousness (Jeremiah 33:16).

As the hymn writer of "On Christ the Solid Rock I Stand" says, all Christians are "dressed in His righteousness alone, faultless to stand before the throne." So is this a promise for all believers? If so, why are so few "flourishing" in their faith? There are two kinds of righteousness: spiritual righteousness and moral righteousness. Spiritual righteousness is our standing before God. Paul was plain at this point, saying that the Lord Jesus "became for us wisdom . . . and righteousness" (1 Corinthians 1:30). Does this mean then that all believers are righteous to the extent that they can "flourish like a palm tree"? If you think you can disobey your parents, cheat on your spouse, steal from your employer, break fellowship with your friends, and expect to "flourish" in your faith, you are sadly mistaken.

It is moral righteousness that is in play here. John made this clear in his first recorded letter: "Little children, let no one deceive you. He who practices righteousness is righteous" (1 John 3:7). The promise of Psalm 92:12 is not for everyone. It is those who live out their faith in a righteous manner, who "practice righteousness," who are pleasing to God.

THE POTENTIAL DISCOVERED

Secondly, we find the *potential discovered*. What is the promise given to one who "practices righteousness"? He will "flourish." What a promised potential is ours! To "flourish"

> In the Christian life we sprout, then we grow, then we thrive, and finally we blossom in our faith.

sets in motion a chain reaction. It means to sprout, to grow, to thrive, to blossom. In the Christian life we sprout, then we grow, then we thrive, and finally we blossom in our faith. All that is wrapped up in the promise God gives to those of us who "practice righteousness."

We search for purpose and peace in so many places and practices. But these are the fruits of a much deeper root. It is not our performance for Christ but our position in Christ that enables us to "flourish like a palm tree." No wonder Jesus said, "Seek first the kingdom of God and His righteousness, and all these things shall be added to you" (Matthew 6:33).

THE PICTURE DETAILED

This promise for us to flourish is accompanied by the *picture detailed*. "The righteous man shall flourish like a palm tree." Out of over 60,000 species of trees, why would the Lord choose the palm tree to picture how the righteous person flourishes?

The palm tree is a fruit-bearing tree, and it bears its fruit all year long, not simply seasonally. The righteous person is like the palm tree in this respect. He or she is "ready in season and out of season" (2 Timothy 4:2) and is consistent in faith, bearing fruit that remains throughout the year.

The palm tree was always a blessing. Many a weary and thirsty traveler journeying across an arid desert knew that when a palm tree became visible on the horizon a refreshing oasis was nearby. The palm tree would mean shade from the scorching sun. There are myriad ways in which the palm tree can be a blessing. The righteous person is like that. When he or she comes in contact with others, they are always a blessing, lightening others' loads and brightening others' roads.

The palm tree has the ability to weather the most ferocious storms. Think about where they grow and thrive. They are found in tropical areas where hurricanes and high winds are always likely possibilities. A palm tree may bend but it does not break. The righteous are not immune to storms of life that beat on us from time to time. But there comes with those storms the supernatural ability to weather them, maybe to bend a bit, but never to break.

Finally, the palm tree has a way of turning what is bitter into what is sweet. Palm trees are often found in the terrain near saltwater. They have their own way of being nurtured by the brackish, bitter saltwater and turning it into delicious and sweet date palms. The righteous man may experience some of the most bitter experiences of life but, at the same time, turn them into blessings for themselves and others.

God has a promise for you. You have the potential to

flourish like a palm tree if—by standing in Christ's own righteousness—you "practice righteousness."

—————— A PROMISE AND A PRAYER ——————

*"Seek first the kingdom of God and His righteousness,
and all these things shall be added to you."*
MATTHEW 6:33

Lord, You know my heart: I want to bear fruit, be a blessing, weather the storms of life, and be able to turn bitterness into blessing. I desire to flourish for Your glory. Thank You that "Christ in me" is my only hope of glory. In Jesus' name, amen.

24

THE PROMISE OF DIRECTION IN LIFE

Trust in the LORD with all your heart, and lean
not on your own understanding; in all your ways
acknowledge Him, and He shall direct your paths.

—PROVERBS 3:5–6

*T*oday's verse is one of the most often-quoted promises in all the Bible. These verses have escaped the lips of children in Vacation Bible Schools, of teenagers in high school graduation speeches, of rugged athletes in professional football Hall of Fame acceptances, and by most all of us from one time or another. It is an amazing promise. If, in our quest to know the path of life we should take, we will simply trust the Lord and not rely solely on ourselves and not be timid to acknowledge His lordship and leadership, then He will lead us along the pathway of life in the direction we should go.

Since trusting and acknowledging the Lord is vital to this quest, Solomon continued to pinpoint the most tangible and tried way we can prove our trust and loyalty to the Lord. Too many of us, in seeking to understand and apply this Bible promise, stop reading in verse six with the *promise*, while verses nine through ten provide the *proof* we need that makes the promise a reality. The writer continued: "Honor the LORD with your possessions, and with the firstfruits of all your increase; so your barns will be filled with plenty, and your vats will overflow with new wine." Your ability to "trust" the Lord and "acknowledge" Him with your possessions is the key to laying hold of His promise. As far-fetched as it might seem, your finances generally mark the position of your spiritual pilgrimage in the arena of trusting Him. Solomon knew you and I would be no further along in our walk with God than the point in which we have learned to trust and acknowledge Him with our possessions. Hence, he planted this promise in the middle of the context of our possessions.

> Your finances generally mark the position of your spiritual pilgrimage in the arena of trusting Him.

Money consumes many of us in our current culture. An abundance of counselors are standing by to give advice. In today's world we are bombarded by financial planners, stock-brokers, bankers, investment gurus, and others all vying for the opportunity to take what is ours and make it grow—for a fee of course. But what if you could get the free counsel of a man recognized the world over as not only one of the wisest men who ever lived but also one of the most successful of all time in the accumulation of wealth? In fact, this man wrote the book on international commerce. Of him it was said he had "great understanding, and largeness of heart like the sand of the seashore . . . [his] wisdom excelled the wisdom of all the men of the East . . . he was wiser than all men" (1 Kings 4:29–31). His name? Solomon, the very one who left us this promise that God would "direct" our paths. And his sage advice? "Honor the LORD with your possessions . . . the firstfruits of all your increase."

THE PURPOSE

Our ability to claim this promise rests on the answers to three questions. First, *What is the* purpose *behind the stewardship of my possessions?* The simple answer is found in the first three words of Proverbs 3:9: "Honor the LORD." This should be your single most important goal in life as a believer. Motivation is a telling factor in our stewardship. Some give because they are motivated by *guilt*. They give because they know they ought to do so. Others are motivated by *grudge*. These people give because they feel like they have to do so. And then there are those who find God's promise because they are motivated by *grace*. That is, they give out of deep appreciation and love for God and because they want to do so. In this way, they honor the Lord.

THE PRODUCT

There is a second question to be asked: *What is the* product *in our stewardship?* Solomon continued, "Honor the LORD with your possessions." Note the pointed product showing the proof that we "trust in the LORD." It is not with our time, nor our talents, but our treasures, our possessions, our "things," our money. We are nothing more than stewards. For most reading these words today, fifty years from now everything you own will be in someone else's name—your home, your land, your stock portfolio, all your assets. In reality, none of that belongs to us. We are simply stewards, and the ability we have to trust God with our possessions is vital to claiming the promise of Proverbs 3:5–6. It is not a coincidence that Solomon added, "with the firstfruits of all your increase."

> The first part of our income is different from all the rest. It belongs to God.

The Bible calls the tithe "holy." The first part of our income is different from all the rest. It belongs to God. Personally, I have never felt that in being so blessed to live in this dispensation of grace, I should give less than the Jews were instructed to give under the law.

THE PROMISE

There is a final question: *What is the* promise *attached to being a good steward of my possessions?* "Your barns will be filled with plenty, and your vats will overflow with new wine." If you are thinking, "Well, I am not sure about that," it is most likely because you have never really tried it. It is worth noting that whenever God speaks to us about our stewardship in the Bible, His emphasis is not on our giving but always on our receiving! He is a good God who delights in delivering His promises to His children when they are faithful to His concerns and commands.

We have and hold a sacred promise: "Trust in the LORD with all your heart, and lean not on your own understanding; in all your ways acknowledge Him, and He shall direct your paths." This is our text. But a text without a context is often nothing more than a pretext. Thus, wise Solomon added, "Honor the LORD with your possessions." He knew that for you and me the real test of being able to claim this promise was in our ability to trust Him with our possessions.

A PROMISE AND A PRAYER

"Those who honor Me I will honor."
1 SAMUEL 2:30

Lord, I climb on this promise today and trust You with all my heart to make known to me the path of life, knowing that in Your presence is found true and lasting joy. In Jesus' name, amen.

25 THE PROMISE OF PLEASURES FOREVERMORE

You will show me the path of life; in Your presence is fullness
of joy; at Your right hand are pleasures forevermore.

—PSALM 16:11

God has His own purpose and His own plan for each of His children. Jesus' passion during His own earthly pilgrimage was to do His Father's will. Once, in the middle of the day at a Samaritan well in Sychar, He testified that the thing that sustained Him on the path of life's journey was being where the Father wanted Him to be and doing what the Father wanted Him to do. He said, "My food is to do the will of Him who sent Me, and to finish His work" (John 4:34). For our Lord, nothing was more important than finding the direction in which He should go and following it. At the end of His life, as the shadows began to fall from the ancient olive trees over Gethsemane's garden, He knelt and prayed, "Not My will, but Yours, be done" (Luke 22:42). Earlier, He had pointedly addressed this passion with His disciples by saying, "I have come down from heaven, not to do My own will, but the will of Him who sent Me" (John 6:38).

If Christ lived with a passion for direction in life, how much more should we? We already have the promise of God's

direction for our own lives. He promised that He would "make known the path of life" for each of us. We are not a group, nor a collection of saints. We are individuals, with unique fingerprints and DNA, who are each, in our own way, indescribably valuable to God. Somewhere there is something you can do that no one else can do quite like you can. God has a path, a direction for you to take, and when you find it and walk in it you have an additional promise of "fullness of joy" accompanied by "pleasures forevermore." Who

of us could not use a little more of that kind of fullness in our lives? The Lord is more interested in your finding His will for your life than you are yourself. To find God's direction, then to walk in it, requires three consecutive steps.

> The Lord is more interested in your finding His will for your life than you are yourself.

STEP ONE

It is impossible to find God's direction in life if we have never come to a saving knowledge of Him, resulting in His Spirit coming to take up residence in our lives. The apostle Paul made this crystal clear in his first letter to his young friend Timothy: "For this is good and acceptable in the sight of God our Savior, who desires all men to be saved and to come to the knowledge of the truth" (1 Timothy 2:3–4). It is impossible for anyone to find direction in life without a

saving knowledge of Christ and His abiding life within. To find God's direction in life demands that it is "spiritually discerned" (1 Corinthians 2:14). So, the first step is to make sure you know Christ in the sense and assurance of His being your personal Savior. This step is made possible by His grace and through your faith (see Ephesians 2:8–9).

STEP TWO

The miracle of the new birth is that once we trust in Christ, God sends His Holy Spirit to live in us, to think through our minds, to live through our lives. This is why Paul admonished the Ephesians to "not be unwise, but understand what the will of the Lord is . . . be filled with the Spirit" (Ephesians 5:17–18). The Holy Spirit living in us becomes the one who will "guide you into all truth" (John 16:13). It is impossible to find direction in life without the leading of God's Spirit in our lives.

STEP THREE

Once we know Christ and the Holy Spirit lives in us, we find God's direction in our lives through a knowledge of biblical truth. God will never set you out on a path that runs contrary to His revealed and recorded Word. It is no wonder Paul admonished those in Colossae to "let the word of Christ dwell in you richly in all wisdom" (Colossians 3:16). When

we know Christ as our personal Savior, when we are being controlled by His Spirit living within us, and when we are abiding in His Word that He has left us, we can hold to His promise that He "will make known to us the path of life."

THE DESIRE IN YOUR HEART

Accompanying these three steps to finding God's direction in life is a very important word: *desire*. God will not lead you in a certain direction without first planting a desire in your heart to go in that way (see Psalm 37:4). For those who know Christ, have the Spirit's leading, and are immersed in His Word, He will be the One who has implanted those very desires in your heart. God does not want to veil His path and plan for you. He is far more desirous of you finding it and walking in it than you are yourself.

God has a plan, a path, a direction for you to go in life where along the way you will find fullness of joy. Pause a moment and recall the first day you came to know Him. (If you don't believe you've come to know Him yet, go to the epilogue right now without reading another word and see how you can come to know Him this very minute.) Yield to His Spirit and search His Word, because so often we find His promises to us right there in

> God has a plan, a path, a direction for you to go in life where along the way you will find fullness of joy.

black and white, on the printed pages of the Bible. Finally, join Jesus in praying, "Not my will but Yours be done." Now, you can join King David in claiming this promise: "You will show me the path of life; in Your presence is fullness of joy; at your right hand are pleasures forevermore" (Psalm 16:11).

— A PROMISE AND A PRAYER —

The natural man does not receive the things of the Spirit of God, for they are foolishness to him; nor can he know them, because they are spiritually discerned.
1 CORINTHIANS 2:14

Lord, You promised You will make known to me the path of life. Guide me now through Your Scriptures and by Your Spirit. Not my way . . . not my will . . . but Your way . . . Your will be done—and right now. In Jesus' name, amen.

26 THE PROMISE OF EVERLASTING LIFE

For God so loved the world that He gave His only begotten Son, that whoever believes in Him should not perish but have everlasting life.
—JOHN 3:16

*I*t is safe to say that the first Bible promise most believers ever heard, or ever memorized, is John 3:16, with its promise of salvation and everlasting life to any and all who would believe in Him. It is the single verse of all the 31,102 verses in the Bible that can be recalled by anyone who knows anything of the Scriptures. These beautifully framed words are most often heard in the innocence and simplicity of a child's voice proudly reciting this promise from memory. These same words are often whispered through the parched lips of an older saint breathing a final breath. This one single verse has often been called the entire gospel in a nutshell.

This old and most often repeated Bible promise tells us much about our own salvation. The motivating factor behind God's redemptive plan for every man and woman He has created is His love for us. He doesn't just love us—He "so" loves us! Paul, in a feeble attempt to express God's love, spoke of its "breadth, and length, and depth, and height" (Ephesians 3:18 KJV). John simply defined Him by saying, "God is love"

(1 John 4:16). God stretches His hand of redemption out to us not because of any good thing we may have done or any high achievements we may have made but expressly because He is motivated by His love for us, regardless of who we are or what we have done. God loves you.

However, His love is not cheap. This Bible promise of eternal life does not come our way without cost. His love for you is so real and so deep that "He gave His only begotten Son" to die for your sins. Only love can do that. In fact, from the very beginning of recorded revelation in the early chapters of Genesis, we find a scarlet thread of redemption that is woven through the Scriptures, coming to fruition in the final and complete sacrifice for sin made on a Roman cross of execution outside the city gates of Jerusalem. Jesus did not simply speak trite platitudes of love; He "demonstrates His own love toward us, in that while we were still sinners, Christ died for us" (Romans 5:8). To claim this promise of salvation for your very own acknowledges that it came at a great cost. "For God so loved the world that He gave His only begotten Son."

> This Bible promise of eternal life does not come our way without cost.

Many have the erroneous idea that to find God's favor we can earn our salvation by doing certain things and by not doing certain other things. But John 3:16 makes it plain that our salvation has already been purchased for us. It is a done deal. We don't deserve it. We can't earn it. We are to "believe in Him." God has done His part. Our part is to believe, to transfer our trust from ourselves and our own efforts to Christ alone and His finished work on the cross. To believe does not mean to give intellectual assent to the claims of Christ. In fact, the Bible says the demons "believe—and tremble" (James 2:19). In another chapter in this volume, we noted the most pointed question in the Bible, asked in the midnight hour by a jailer: "What must I do to be saved?" (Acts 16:30). In a flash came the one-sentence reply from Paul: "Believe on the Lord Jesus Christ, and you will be saved" (Acts 16:31). Salvation is the free gift of God's grace to all who will "believe."

Now follows the promise to you, to me, to any and all who believe: we will "not perish but have everlasting life." Those without Christ are "perishing." A visiting preacher was walking with an interpreter down a Mexican street when he spotted a sign that appeared to be a Bible verse written in Spanish. Asking his interpreter to read the sign, he translated John 3:16 in the following way, "God loved the world so very much that He gave His only Son that if you believe in Him you will not lose any more of your life but gain life eternal." Did you catch that? You "will not lose any more of your life." Those who have not found new life in Christ are perishing—they are losing a little more of their lives each day that cannot be claimed for Christ.

The promise of salvation, of "everlasting life," is for those who realize that God's love reaches down to where they are, that His salvation has been made possible through the death of Christ on the cross, and who believe in Him. Those in Christ never die. They live forever throughout the endless ages of eternity. When they breathe their last breath and their heart beats its last beat, they become more alive than they have ever been and enter a dimension where "God will wipe away every tear from their eyes; there shall be no more death, nor sorrow, nor crying. There shall be no more pain, for the former things have passed away" (Revelation 21:4). What a place. What a promise. What a Savior.

> Those in Christ never die. They live forever throughout the endless ages of eternity.

I'll say it again: "For God so loved the world that He gave His only begotten Son, that whoever believes in Him should not perish but have everlasting life." Yes, God knows you . . . God loves you . . . and He has a wonderful plan for your life. The promise of salvation is yours for the asking.

A PROMISE AND A PRAYER

God demonstrates His own love toward us, in that
while we were still sinners, Christ died for us.
ROMANS 5:8

Lord, immerse me in Your unconditional love. No one
has ever loved me, nor will anyone ever love me, the way
You love me right now. I believe—help my unbelief. In
Jesus' name, amen.

27 THE PROMISE OF A SUCCESSFUL LIFE

"This Book of the Law shall not depart from your mouth, but
you shall meditate in it day and night, that you may observe to
do according to all that is written in it. For then you will make
your way prosperous, and then you will have good success."

—JOSHUA 1:8

*S*uccess is one of those words that is viewed in a contradictory sense by many in the Christian world today. For some it carries with it the idea of accumulated possessions or aspiring positions. But in God's economy, He desires for His followers to be successful in the purest sense of the word, which is to find the will of God for your life and then to do it. His will for Joshua was for him to have "good success." Nehemiah returned from Babylonian captivity to rebuild the broken walls of Jerusalem with this promise: "The God of heaven will give us success" (Nehemiah 2:20 NIV). It is said of Joseph, "The LORD was with Joseph, and he was a successful man" (Genesis 39:2). The Lord does not define success in the way the world does. In the promise of this chapter we find that success is conditional on two emphases related to His Word. Successful people, in God's eyes, are those who *read it* and those who *heed it*.

After forty long and tedious years of wilderness wanderings, the Israelites stood on the eastern bank of the Jordan River with their goal of Canaan in sight, just across the river. As they were about to embark into the promised land, God turned their attention to His Word, admonishing them to "meditate on it day and night" and "do according to all that is written in it." Then, and only then, would they know true and lasting success in their land of promised blessing.

READ YOUR BIBLE

The first step toward spiritual success is to *read it*. Your Bible is of little use to you if it simply sits on your coffee table or nightstand and is dusted along with the furniture every so often. The promise of success in life is predicated by our opening God's Word daily and "meditating on it day and night." This word to Joshua was a high-water mark in Christian growth. No one ever before had been instructed to get his marching orders from God through the words of a book. Abraham obeyed God's voice when he left Ur of the Chaldeans. He had no book to read and heed. Joseph received God's revelation through his dreams. Moses heard God's voice speaking to him through a burning bush (Genesis 12:1, 4; 37:5–10; Exodus 3:2, respectively).

Moses was now dead. But he had left Joshua the books of the law, which he had received from God—Genesis,

Exodus, Leviticus, Numbers, and Deuteronomy. Thus Joshua became the first man to learn the will and way of God through the words of God in a book in the same way we do today.

> Success is promised to those of us who read the Word today, who "meditate" on it as a constant daily practice

Success is promised to those of us who read the Word today, who "meditate" on it as a constant daily practice so that it begins to penetrate our thinking process and leads us in the way we should go. Your Bible cannot do this for you—unless you *read it*!

HEED THE WORDS OF THE BIBLE

However, success does not come only by our reading of the Bible. Secondly, we are to *heed it*. We are to "do" according to all that is written in the pages between its covers. Reading the Bible gives us a knowledge *about* God. Since knowledge is the accumulation of facts, most people can acquire knowledge if they stay in the library long enough. Obeying the Bible is what enables us to have a knowledge *of* God. My problem is not in knowing what the Bible says I should do; it is actually doing it. Many of us obey the Word—but only partially. We have our own ways of picking and choosing what we want to obey and what we conveniently ignore.

Joshua's call is to "do according to *all* that is written" in the Word of God.

HAVE GOOD SUCCESS

There is in our text an important four-letter word: *then*. When we read and heed the Word, *then* we will have "good success." We do this through a consistent and constant daily practice of reading and meditating on God's Word, keeping it in our hearts, and letting it permeate our very being so that it guides the thought processes of our minds, resulting in our walking in obedience. Like the psalmist, we will begin to find our joy and delight in reading the Word and meditating on it "day and night" (Psalm 1:2).

True success in life is to stay in the Word of God until we find the *will* of God so that we can *walk* in the *ways* of God. The Word. The Will. The Walk. The Way. At the wedding feast in Cana where Jesus performed His first miracle, Mary left us one of the most valuable life lessons we could ever learn when she simply said, "Whatever [Jesus] says to you, *do it*" (John 2:5, emphasis added).

Success in life is the ability to find God's will for your life and to do it. He has left us His final Word on the subject. We call it the Bible. Read it. And then don't forget to heed it—and "then you will have good success."

A PROMISE AND A PRAYER

Blessed is the man who walks not in the counsel of the ungodly . . .
his delight is in the law of the LORD, and in His law he meditates
day and night . . . and whatever he does shall prosper.

PSALM 1:1–3

Lord, as I open Your Word, show me Your will and way
and lead me to walk in it today. In Jesus' name, amen.

28 THE PROMISE OF SECURITY

Being confident of this very thing, that He who has begun a good
work in you will complete it until the day of Jesus Christ.
—PHILIPPIANS 1:6

*P*aul could be confident in what he said and recorded
for all posterity because he recognized the true origin
of his salvation and, consequently, could rest in the outcome
of it. Many personal testimonies of salvation follow this line:
"I heard the gospel. I decided to follow Jesus. I came to Him.
I opened my heart to Him. I received Him. I repented of my
sin." Note the constant use of the perpendicular pronoun *I*,
as if it all depended on me and what I did. When we all get
to heaven, I suspect some are going to be surprised to learn
how very little they actually had to do with their own salvation and how true it is that He is the
One who had actually "begun a good
work" in us. Salvation is from first to
last, from beginning to end, from start
to finish, the work of the Lord Jesus
Himself in us. He found us; we did not
find Him. He began the good work in
us; we did not take the initiative. He
keeps us eternally secure; it is not about

> When we all get to
> heaven, I suspect
> some are going
> to be surprised to
> learn how very little
> they actually had
> to do with their
> own salvation.

our trying to hold on until the end. And He is the One who will one day present us faultless before His Father's throne in glory. After all, it was the shepherd who went after the one lost sheep until he found it, then put it on his shoulders and carried it back to the fold (Luke 15:1–7). Getting home safely and securely depended on the shepherd and not the sheep.

RECOGNIZING THE ORIGIN OF OUR SALVATION

Confidence comes when we *recognize the origin of our salvation*. The Lord is the One who began the good work in you. You say, "I thought I did. I took the initiative. I thought I repented. I thought I came to Christ." No, God did the work. And when we recognize this fact, we can find rest in the promise of our own security in Christ.

We were all *unresponsive* to the gospel message. The Bible reveals we were "dead" in our sins (Romans 6:11). But that is not all. We were also *unperceptive*. The gospel was "veiled" to us and the devil had "blinded" us to the truth so that we could not believe on our own (2 Corinthians 4:3–4). And, as if that were not enough, the Bible explains that we were also *unteachable*. We considered the things of God "foolishness," and we could not understand them because they are "spiritually discerned" (1 Corinthians 2:14). Finally, in our natural state we were *unrighteous*. We were actually shaped in iniquity and conceived in sin (Psalm 51:5). Yes, "all we like sheep" have gone astray wandering aimlessly of our own accord (Isaiah 53:6).

Since being unresponsive, unperceptive, unteachable, and unrighteous is the condition of each of us in our natural state without Christ, something outside of us must intervene to enable us to become responsive to the gospel, perceptive of the things of God, teachable, and righteous in our standing before Him. This is exactly what our text with its promise of security says: "He who has begun a good work in you." The origin of our salvation lies not within us but with God Himself. He is the initiator, the One who begins the good work of salvation. He convicts of sin. He convinces of righteousness. He calls us unto Himself, out of our darkness into His marvelous light.

> The origin of our salvation lies not within us but with God Himself.

RESTING IN THE OUTCOME OF OUR SALVATION

Confidence continues when we *rest in the outcome of our salvation*. What a precious promise of security: He "will complete [the good work] until the day of Jesus Christ." We can be secure in the *now* life. Christ, who Himself began this good work, promised to "complete" it. He will never let us go.

> If faith alone is good enough to save us, it is good enough to live by and to keep us.

Since we cannot be saved by performing good works, we are not kept secure by performing good works. Paul said, "As you therefore have received Christ Jesus the Lord, so walk in Him" (Colossians 2:6). If faith alone is good enough to save us, it is good enough to live by and to keep us.

When Wendy, our firstborn, was learning to walk, she would reach up with her chubby little fingers and hold tight to my index finger, hanging on with all her might. After a couple of steps she would let go of my finger and fall flat on her bottom on the ground. It did not take me long to learn an important lesson every parent has learned. I reached down and grabbed hold of her little hand myself and held it tight. Then, when she invariably stumbled, I was there to hold her up and keep her from falling. In just this way our security in Christ is not a matter of our holding on as best we can until the bitter end. God reaches down to us and grabs us with His own hand. And when we stumble, as we so often do, He is there to hold us up and keep us from falling. We are secure right now in Him.

We are not just secure in the *now* life but in the *next* life as well. This promise of security in Christ endures until "the day of Christ Jesus." This describes that coming grand and glorious day when He will return to receive us as His own.

On that day, the church, you and me, the "body of Christ," will become the "bride of Christ." Jesus declared, "This is the will of the Father who sent Me, that of all He has given Me I should lose nothing, but should raise it up at the last day" (John 6:39).

This promise should bring a sense of security to every believer: "He who has begun a good work in you will complete it until the day of Jesus Christ" (Philippians 1:6). Since He is the origin of it all, you can trust Him with the outcome of it all. No wonder we sing, "Blessed assurance, Jesus is mine!"

A PROMISE AND A PRAYER

"My sheep hear My voice, and I know them, and they follow Me. And I give them eternal life, and they shall never perish; neither shall anyone snatch them out of My hand."
JOHN 10:27–28

Lord, I rest now in Your promise that nothing can separate me from Your love. Thank You that I can know that I am eternally secure in You—all the way until "that day" and beyond, through the endless ages of eternity in the next life. In Jesus' name, amen.

29 THE PROMISE OF REDEMPTION

In Him we have redemption through His blood, the
forgiveness of sins, according to the riches of His grace.
—EPHESIANS 1:7

*I*n Him *we have redemption*." What a promise to know that we do not have to hope for redemption or wish for it, but that we have it right now "in Him." I never will forget the first time I saw or heard this word, *redemption*. As a small boy I dreamed of having a genuine leather baseball glove to replace my vinyl one as I joined the neighborhood kids on the old vacant lot on our street for our afternoon ball games. In those long-ago days, no one had credit cards with which to earn points in order to redeem certain gifts. No one I knew flew on airplanes, and the airlines had not yet initiated their mileage program whereby free trips or other merchandise could be redeemed and used. But we had the forerunner to all of this, something most people have not even heard of in our day: S&H green stamps!

For every dollar you spent at the grocery store, gas station, or other businesses, you received these stamps that you saved and could later exchange for various pieces of merchandise. I discovered in my mother's catalog that for two and a

half books of green stamps I could earn a genuine leather ball glove. She let me have the green stamps she received from her various shopping excursions, and I was on my way to filling up those two and a half books with those little green stamps. Weeks turned into months and finally, after what seemed like forever, I had filled the books with the required amount. I brought the magazine to the dinner table that night with the books of green stamps and asked my dad what the next step might be. He informed me that the coming Saturday he would take me to exchange the green stamps for the glove I so longed to have. I lived for that Saturday.

> I discovered in my mother's catalog that for two and a half books of green stamps I could earn a genuine leather ball glove.

On the appointed day we drove from our home on the east side of Fort Worth to the south side of town. We turned off McCart Street and pulled into the parking lot where there was a large, whitewashed, concrete-block building. As we exited the car and began to walk toward the building, I noticed a large sign over the door: "S&H Green Stamp *Redemption* Center." It was the first time I had ever seen or heard of that word—*redemption*. But I found out its meaning that day. Upon entering the building, I walked up to the counter, showed the lady the ball glove in the magazine, and placed the two and a half books of green stamps beside it.

She disappeared into a back room and emerged with a square box that she pushed across the counter toward me. When I got back in the car, I pulled the treasured glove out of its box, put it on my left hand, and with a right fist punched the pocket of the glove all the way home. A teenager up the street told me to get some linseed oil, rub it in the glove's pocket, put a ball in there, and wrap large rubber bands around it to form the pocket. I slept with that glove the first few nights I had it. I had redeemed my new ball glove with two and a half books of S&H green stamps.

And so, one day our Lord stepped up to redemption's counter. His Father sent Him. Down He came, past solar systems, constellations, and through measureless space. Down still farther to be born in the filth of a Bethlehem stable where sickness, disease, and even death were likely possibilities. Down further to be misunderstood, mocked, beaten, and spit on. Down still further to be nailed to a Roman cross of execution where He stepped up to redemption's counter and put down His own blood. Why? So He could take you home with Him!

This is the promise of the gospel—"in *Him*" we have redemption. What Christ has to offer us is not in religion or in some ritual but in a vital, living, personal relationship with Him. It is "in

> This is the promise of the gospel—"in *Him*" we have redemption

Him." Many today are on a search for a meaningful relationship. The most meaningful relationship we can ever know is in coming into relationship with Christ, for it is "in Him," and in Him alone, we find redemption.

This promised redemption came at a great price. "In Him we have redemption *through His blood.*" Since our redemption has already been purchased for us, there is nothing we can do to earn or deserve it. It is the free gift of eternal life. Jesus didn't go to the cross and put a little down of His blood as payment for our sins so that we have to work our own way to redemption. He paid our debt in full—"through His blood."

And the result of all this? "*The forgiveness of sins,* according to the riches of His grace." Our promised and purchased redemption through the blood of Christ is what wipes our slates clean and forgives us of our sins, according to the riches of His grace. There is no more beautiful word than that one: *grace.* God is rich in His mercy and grace toward us. Yes, "for you know the grace of our Lord Jesus Christ, that though He was rich, yet for your sakes He became poor, that you through His poverty might become rich" (2 Corinthians 8:9).

> There is no more beautiful word than that one: *grace.*

God has purchased and promised our redemption. What Christ has to offer us is for right now, not just some hope of

heaven in the future. "We have redemption." We live in a world of immediate gratification. We don't want to have to wait for anything. "Give it to me, and give it to me right now" is the cry of so many. Come to Jesus, surrender to His lordship, and you will know immediate gratification that never ends. Why? Because "in Him we have redemption through His blood, the forgiveness of sins, according to the riches of His grace."

A PROMISE AND A PRAYER

You were not redeemed with corruptible things, like silver or gold, from your aimless conduct received by tradition from your fathers, but with the precious blood of Christ, as of a lamb without blemish and without spot.
1 PETER 1:18–19

Lord, thank You for Your blood that made a way out of no way for me when You placed it at the altar of the cross to redeem me to Yourself. Help me to walk worthy of this tremendous price today. In Jesus' name, amen.

30 THE PROMISE OF HEAVEN

"In My Father's house are many mansions; if it were not so,
I would have told you. I go to prepare a place for you."

—JOHN 14:2

The atmosphere in the upper room on Mount Zion that evening took on the mood of confusion and uncertainty. Within a couple of hours their leader and Lord would be arrested, brutally beaten, and within a day would be hanging on a Roman cross of execution outside the city walls of Jerusalem. Looking into the troubled faces of those who had lived with Him and learned from Him for over three years as they traversed the hills of Galilee and the deserts of Judea, He began by saying, "Let not your heart be troubled; you believe in God, believe also in Me" (John 14:1). There was a reason for them to be comforted by these words. He went on to tell them He was going to leave them, that He was going on before them to "prepare a place" for them in heaven so that where He was, there they could also dwell throughout the endless ages of eternity—with Him, in a place called heaven.

We live in a world where an increasing number of people even in the church

> We live in a world where an increasing number of people even in the church world do not believe in an eternal hell.

world do not believe in an eternal hell, a place of everlasting punishment. Frequently, we hear, "How could a loving God allow anyone to go to hell regardless of what they may have done and didn't do?" My problem has always been just the opposite. By that I mean, how could there be such a wonderful place like heaven described in the Bible? How could the love and grace of God be so awesome as to make it possible for a sinner like me to spend eternity in such a place?

From his lonely island of exile, John saw "a door standing open in heaven" (Revelation 4:1). God has left us a few "open doors" in the Scriptures that enable us to peek inside the pearly gates and catch a glimpse of what awaits us there. To begin with, heaven is a real place. Jesus said, "I go to prepare a *place* for you." Throughout human history God has implanted within the heart of man a longing for such a place. In the ancient past, cave dwellers depicted with paintings on the walls of their caves a belief in some sort of afterlife. More than three millennia ago the Egyptians, in great pomp and circumstance, buried their pharaohs with supplies, weapons, even servants in their quest for a life that was somewhere out there beyond this present one. The American Indians had their own "happy hunting grounds" where they held to the hope that their departed lived again. God has implanted within the soul of every man a longing and a desire for more than this life has to offer.

This longing has never been more prevalent than in our day. Every time a scientist enters the lab in search of a cure for cancer, it is an expression of a subconscious hunger for a world free of disease and pain. Heaven is such a place. Every time a social worker strives to eliminate rancid living conditions, it is an expression of a desire for a world without poverty and homelessness. Heaven is such a place. Every environmentalist on a quest to obtain clean water and a pure environment is an expression of a world that is pure and beautiful. Heaven is such a place. World leaders sitting at peace conferences in hot spots around the world are simply expressing an inner desire for a world without war and conflict. Heaven is such a place. We need a place called heaven, and heaven alone must fulfill what we leave unfinished here.

> We need a place called heaven, and heaven alone must fulfill what we leave unfinished here.

But heaven is not simply a place; it is a *prepared* place. It is beautiful. God loves beauty or He would not have made things on this sin-cursed world so beautiful. John got a glimpse of it and wrote, "Its wall was of jasper; and the city was pure gold, like clear glass" (Revelation 21:18). It is no wonder that earlier the inspired apostle Paul had said, "Eye has not seen, nor ear heard, nor have entered into the heart of man the things which God has prepared for those who love Him" (1 Corinthians 2:9).

When we walk the streets of this "prepared place," there are some things we will never see. We will never see a hospital. There is no more sickness. We will never see a counseling center. There is no depression or mental illness there. We will never see a funeral home because there is no more death. We will never see a police station. There is no crime there. There will be no courthouses in heaven. There will be no lawsuits there. We will never be awakened by the shrill sound of an ambulance. There will be no more emergencies. Because there is no fear, we will never lock our homes. There will be no handicapped parking places, no ramps for wheelchairs, and no nursing homes because we will never grow old. What a place it must be that Jesus is preparing for us!

Heaven will also be a place of reward. The Bible speaks of many crowns that will be given to believers. But we will not parade up and down the golden streets showing them off. We will take our crowns and cast them at the feet of the only One who is worthy, the Lord Jesus Christ.

Many seem to have the idea that heaven is a long way away. Not really. You are only one heartbeat away. And one of these coming days, that heart of yours—and mine—is going to stop. Then, in the wink of an eye, we will step over into eternity . . . somewhere. Because of Jesus' promise, those of us who know Christ as our personal Savior will begin the great adventure of living in a place called heaven, forever and forever.

A PROMISE AND A PRAYER

For our citizenship is in heaven, from which we also
eagerly wait for the Savior, the Lord Jesus Christ.
PHILIPPIANS 3:20

Lord, when I hear of aliens in the news, I am reminded
that I am an alien myself. I am a citizen of the kingdom of
heaven, simply passing through on my way home. Thank
You for "preparing a place" for me there. In Jesus' name,
amen.

31 THE PROMISE OF REJOICING

*Those who sow in tears shall reap in joy. He who continually
goes forth weeping, bearing seed for sowing, shall doubtless
come again with rejoicing, bringing his sheaves with him.*

—PSALM 126:5–6

On July 27, 1981, a hot summer day, our city of Fort
Lauderdale came to a shocking halt, and all attention
was focused on finding a little six-year-old boy, the age of our
own daughter. He had gone missing from a Sears department
store we ourselves had frequented on numerous occasions.
Adam Walsh caught the attention of an entire nation as
thousands volunteered in the search for this lost child. The
tragic saga ended sixteen days later with the realization that
an abductor had snatched him away, when his remains were
found in a canal 120 miles away. His father, John Walsh, went
from this horrible experience to dedicating his life to saving
lost and abducted children. Many remember him from his
years of hosting the popular television show, *America's Most
Wanted*.

After moving to Dallas, another child became the focus
of national attention when little Amber Hagerman went missing from a shopping center. Like Adam Walsh, she became
the object of a massive search, again prompting thousands

of volunteers to scour the surrounding area for days in all-out search. Sadly, a few days later her little lifeless body was found near a remote Arlington creek bank. She lives on in our memory today through the national "Amber Alert" system, which seeks to quickly provide information on missing, lost, and abducted children in hopes of their speedy retrieval and recovery.

While these and a multitude of other stories from virtually every city in America are so worthy of our attention and involvement, we who are believers somehow do not seem as urgently concerned about those around us whom Satan has snatched and are spiritually lost. As I type these words, I cannot help but think what would happen if we devoted the same intensity and earnest efforts in going forth "sowing" the seed of the gospel and doing so with tears as the psalmist challenged. Not to mention, when we do go, we have God's promise that we shall "doubtless come again with rejoicing," bringing our sheaves with us.

The more we become like Jesus in our own Christian journey, the more we will become interested in what holds His interest. He expressed the reason for His coming to earth when He said, "For the Son of Man has come to seek and to save that which was lost" (Luke 19:10). I am not certain that many of us really look on those without Christ as lost today. In fact, the word *lost* is one we seldom, if ever, hear spoken in our modern day. We prefer other, more noncontroversial expressions of those without Christ. We refer to them as "unreached people groups." Perhaps the favorite expression used today for those who are lost is *seeker*. But Jesus did not say that He came to seek and to save "unreached people groups" or "seekers." He came to seek out, to search for, and to save those who are "lost." Whisper that word to yourself now. Go ahead—say it: "lost." We need to awaken to the fact that those family members and friends we know who are not Christians are *lost*—lost beyond hope, lost beyond time, lost beyond eternity, lost beyond Christ, *lost*, forever lost without Christ.

> The more we become like Jesus in our own Christian journey, the more we will become interested in what holds His interest.

We have this precious promise from God. When we begin to see our friends as lost, when we become so burdened for their salvation that we weep tears as Jesus wept when He looked over the city of Jerusalem, and when we begin to sow the seeds of the gospel on their hearts, we, too, could know true "rejoicing" as we bring these people to Jesus. They are waiting. But we don't seem to be seeking, much less weeping. Paul made it plain that they are blind to the gospel, saying, "If our gospel be hid, it is hid to them that are lost" (2 Corinthians 4:3 KJV). What a promise is ours: "He who continually goes forth weeping, bearing seed for sowing, shall doubtless come again with rejoicing, bringing his sheaves with him."

I love the certainty of this promise: you shall *doubtless* come again rejoicing. In the often-repeated parable of the lost sheep, Jesus reminded us that when the shepherd eventually found the lost sheep, he exclaimed, "Rejoice with me, for I have found my sheep which was lost!" (Luke 15:6). Then Jesus put his own exclamation point on the truth of Psalm 126:5–6, saying, "I say to you that likewise there will be more joy in heaven over one sinner who repents than over ninety-nine just persons who need no repentance" (Luke 15:7). And to put a capstone on this truth, He concluded what Longfellow called the greatest short story ever written, the parable of the prodigal son, with these words of the father to his eldest son: "It was right that we should make merry and be glad, for your brother was dead and is alive again, and was lost and is found" (Luke 15:32). Yes, when we are faithful in our witness we shall "doubtless" come again, like the shepherd and the father, with rejoicing. They strike up the band in heaven when we go forth "weeping, bearing seed for sowing." And we have His promise, we shall doubtless come again with rejoicing, bringing our sheaves with us.

> I love the certainty of this promise: you shall *doubtless* come again rejoicing.

"Likewise, I say to you, there is joy in the presence of the angels of God over one sinner who repents."

LUKE 15:10

Lord, give me a burden for someone I know who needs to know You. And grant me the grace and courage to spread the seed of Your convicting Word on their heart, that I might know true rejoicing in seeing that person come to You in the free pardoning of sin. In Jesus' name, amen.

32 THE PROMISE FOR PARENTS

Train up a child in the way he should go, and
when he is old he will not depart from it.

—PROVERBS 22:6

*S*ome of the best parents I have known have had kids
grow into young adulthood making some of the
worst choices one could make. On the other hand, some of
the most detached parents I have known have ended up with
some of the most obedient children, often making the nur-
ture of children one of the biggest mysteries of life. Raising
children is among the highest of all stewardships in God's
economy. It comes with an amazing promise that if we train
our children in the proper manner, they will not depart from
the way in which they have been brought up.

Warning: this promise is not for all parents. It has a
prerequisite. We are to "train" them. The promise is not
predicated by our "teaching" them but by our "training"
them. Training a child entails much more than teaching a
child. Training is more caught than taught because those
who train their kids are the ones who model the life they
are teaching before them. The promise continues with the
emphasis on training our children "in the way they should
go." We never have to teach our children to disobey. They

> We never have to teach our children to disobey. They are born with that inclination.

are born with that inclination. We have to teach them to obey—to train them "in the way they should go," not in their own selfish way in which they seek to maneuver and sometimes manipulate us through the growing-up years.

Susie and I raised two daughters in our home who have brought us nothing but joy and happiness across the decades. We never sought to be rigid with them or to give them a list of rules, but to be real before them. We prayed together. But we also spent a lot of time playing together. Like Jesus, who grew "in wisdom and stature, and in favor with God and men" (Luke 2:52), we sought to raise our kids with balance—intellectually, physically, spiritually, and socially. Training our children in the proper way insists that we maintain this balance and not go to seed on any of these four aspirations. Some spend all their time training their children intellectually (in wisdom) with the intent to get them into the best schools. Some go to seed on the physical aspect (stature) of their growth. Still others focus most of their attention on the social growth (favor with men). And it can even be argued that it is possible to get out of balance by only focusing on the spiritual growth of a child (favor with God) so much so that they never develop the social skills needed to carry out Christian witness. Healthy kids are balanced kids, who, like our Lord, are trained to grow in these four distinct areas at the same time.

TEACH YOUR CHILDREN
TO ASK FOR THINGS

To be able to claim this promise for our children's spiritual maturity as they grow older and leave the home, we should "train" them in three important and practical ways. First, we train them by *teaching them to ask for things*. When they are babies crawling on the floor, unable to verbalize their needs, they get attention by crying, screaming, and throwing a fit. A few months later they sit in a highchair and seek to get their way by pointing or throwing food from their plates. When they learn to verbalize their needs with words, they usually try to make demands, saying, "Give me this" or "Give me that." At this point the wise parent begins to train their child to ask for what it is they desire. It sounds simple, but this is the first important step in the training process. Ask.

TEACH YOUR CHILDREN TO SEARCH
OUT THINGS FOR THEMSELVES

Once the child is older and in school, the wise parent then trains the child by *teaching them to search out things for themselves*. As our daughters got older and came to me with

> Wise parents train their children to search out the answer for themselves, to figure it out on their own.

a math problem, asking, for example, "What is six times seven?" I would have done them a disservice by simply giving them all the answers. Wise parents train their children to search out the answers for themselves, to figure them out on their own. Some parents simply gave their kids everything they asked for and sent them out into the world unprepared to have to seek out anything on their own. It is impossible to train our children in the way they should go without first teaching them to act and then to search for themselves.

TEACH YOUR CHILDREN TO NEVER GIVE UP

Finally, those who see this parental promise fulfilled in their children learn that *teaching them not to quit, to never give up* is one of life's most valuable lessons. When the time came to open our hands and let our daughters fly off on their own to their college experience, we made sure that embedded deep within each of them was this spirit of perseverance. Some things would require them simply to ask for an answer. Other times they would need to pay the personal price of searching and seeking the answers for themselves. And, no matter what, they should never give up, give in, or give out.

Training your children is but a microcosm of the way

Jesus trains you and me. Didn't He train us, His children, in the same way? Hear Him on a grassy Galilean mountainside: Ask . . . seek . . . keep on knocking and the door will be opened to you (Matthew 7:7–8). We grow into spiritual maturity in the same way we seek to lead our own children. When we know God's will for our lives, we simply ask. When we are uncertain of His will, we seek until we find it. And, when we are sure of His will but as yet have not seen the answer, we keep knocking with the promise that the door "will be opened" to us.

We parents have a precious promise: "Train up a child in the way he should go, and when he is old he will not depart from it" (Proverbs 22:6). If you have trained your child in such a way, believe this promise, hold to it, "and when he is old he will not depart from it."

A PROMISE AND A PRAYER

"Honor your father and mother," which is the first commandment with promise: "that it may be well with you and you may live long on the earth."
EPHESIANS 6:2–3

Lord, give me Your wisdom in training my children, and help me practice all that I preach, that they may grow, like You, in wisdom, in stature, in favor with God, and in favor with men. In Jesus' name, amen.

33 THE PROMISE OF BLESSING

"Try Me now in this . . . if I will not open for you the
windows of heaven and pour out for you such blessing
that there will not be room enough to receive it."

—MALACHI 3:10

*T*oday's verse contains quite a promise. It is rich in
quality. God calls it a blessing. And it is rich in quantity. God's desire is to fulfill this promise to you in a way that
"there will not be room enough to receive it." But, like many
of His promises, it comes with a caveat. It is preceded and
predicated with the condition that, first, we return the tithe
(one-tenth of our income) to Him. He calls us to "bring all
the tithes into the storehouse" (Malachi 3:10) and then challenges us to prove Him, to put Him to the test, if He will not
be faithful to His word and a keeper of His promise to pour
out His blessing on us. This is one of the only directives in
all the Bible where God calls on us to test Him, to take Him
at His word, regarding His own faithfulness to His promise.

Moses declared that the tithe was "holy to the LORD"
(Leviticus 27:30). There are not a lot of things God calls holy.
The word *holy* means set apart from the rest, different. There
was a room in the Jewish temple called holy; in fact, it was
called the Holy of Holies. That room was different from all

other rooms in the temple. Within its walls no one entered, except the high priest, and then only once a year on the high and holy Day of Atonement. He would enter that room to sprinkle the blood of the sacrifice over the mercy seat of the ark of the covenant. Then the *shekinah* glory of God would fill the room as God came to meet with His people. No one started a game of dominos in that room. No one played volleyball in that room. It was set apart, different from all other rooms. It was holy. The golden vessels used for temple worship were called holy (Ezra 8:27–28). They were different, set apart for the sole use of worship in the temple. No one drank coffee from one of those goblets. They were holy. So, God called the tithe holy in the same way. One-tenth of our income is different from all the rest. It is to be set aside for Him and His use. He considers it holy. No wonder God accuses those who do not tithe of robbery, saying, "You have robbed Me" in tithes and offerings (Malachi 3:9). This is a strong accusation, not a casual insinuation.

> One-tenth of our income is different from all the rest. It is to be set aside for Him and His use.

The stewardship of your possessions is extremely personal with God. Note the use of the personal pronouns: "*You* have robbed *Me*." Jesus instructed us to "render . . . to Caesar the things that are Caesar's, and to God the things that are

God's" (Matthew 22:21). Most believers would never entertain the slightest thought of not paying their income taxes or their property taxes, yet, at the same time, they seldom, if ever, render to God the things that He says are holy and belong to Him, the tithes of His people. Perhaps we live in a day when some of God's own people fear the government more than they do their God.

To those who are faithful in the stewardship of the blessings in which He has entrusted them, He has given the promise that He will pour out His blessings on them in quality and in quantity. Yes, He will "open . . . the windows of heaven and pour out for you such blessing that there will not be room enough to receive it."

As far-fetched as it may seem to some, our finances are often the best indicator of our own spiritual pilgrimage. We are often no farther along in our Christian growth than the point to which we have learned to trust Him with our tithes and offerings. One out of every three parables Jesus told had to do with the stewardship of our income and the blessings with which He has entrusted us. But God's emphasis is never on our giving. He always focuses on our receiving. We find this here in His instructions to tithe. He said, "Bring all the tithes." Why? For the express purpose that He might "open . . . the windows of heaven" and shower us with His blessings, even to the extent that we can no longer contain them. It is not that He needs our money. God owns "the cattle on a thousand hills" (Psalm 50:10). God's desire is to bless those of us who can trust Him, and the more we seem to do this, the more He blesses as He promised.

So God presents us with an amazing promise. But He predicates it: "Bring all the tithes into the storehouse." And then He leaves us with a proposition: "Try Me . . . prove Me . . . put Me to the test." Here is one directive in Scripture that we can put on a trial basis. If there is any doubt as to God's desire to bless you, here is a way to prove it. Abundant blessings await you and me. Get started now. Do it. "'Try Me now in this,' says the LORD of hosts, 'if I will not open for you the windows of heaven and pour out for you such blessing that there will not be room enough to receive it.'"

A PROMISE AND A PRAYER

"Give, and it will be given to you; good measure, pressed down, shaken together, and running over will be put into your bosom. For with the same measure that you use, it will be measured back to you."

LUKE 6:38

Lord, all I have has come from Your hand. As Jacob prayed so long ago, "I will not let you go until You bless me." I open my hand to give to You what You call "holy," and I open my heart to receive Your promised blessing. You are faithful. In Jesus' name, amen.

34 THE PROMISE OF WARNING

"Unless you repent you will all likewise perish."

—LUKE 13:3

Not all of God's promises in the Bible are filled with hope and comfort. Some of them raise certain red warning flags of dangers looming ahead. As these words escaped Jesus' lips, they were not just a statement of fact but more a promise of a severe outcome if a warning went unheeded: "Unless you repent you . . . will perish."

We find this word, *perish*, woven like a thread through the tapestry of the pages of the New Testament. Perhaps it is best remembered in His promise: "For God so loved the world that He gave His only begotten Son, that whoever believes in Him should not *perish* but have everlasting life" (John 3:16). Later in John's gospel, when speaking of His "sheep," Jesus claims, "I give them eternal life, and they shall never *perish*; neither shall anyone snatch them out of My hand" (John 10:28). To the Corinthians, Paul said, "For the message of the cross is foolishness to those who are *perishing*, but to us who are being saved it is the power of God" (1 Corinthians 1:18). Peter also weighed in, saying, "The Lord is not slack concerning His promise . . . not willing that any should *perish* but that all should come to repentance" (2 Peter 3:9).

In the Bible *perish* does not mean to come to nothing or simply to rot away. It carries with it the idea of a horrible existence separated and isolated from all that is good. It has to do with something that is beyond our death—specifically, the coming judgment of God on our sin

> It behooves us to know exactly what repentance entails and how we can apply it to our lives.

resulting in eternal punishment. If repentance is what keeps us from this plight, as Jesus plainly stated in Luke 13:3, then it behooves us to know exactly what repentance entails and how we can apply it to our lives.

Repentance is of such importance that Jesus *commenced* His ministry with this message (Matthew 4:17) and *concluded* His ministry with this same emphasis (Luke 24:46–47). It was the message of John the Baptist as he preached in the wilderness (Matthew 3:1–2). It was the message of the apostles as they scattered across the world preaching (Mark 6:12). Repentance was the message that birthed the church at Pentecost (Acts 2:37–38). It was the missionary message of the apostle Paul (Acts 17:30). And it was the message of John to the seven churches from Patmos, his lonely island of exile (Revelation 2:5).

Before discovering what repentance actually is, it is important to see what it is not. Repentance is not *remorse*, simply being sorry for your sin. The rich young ruler went

> Judas took the thirty pieces of silver back to the priests. He reformed, but he didn't repent (Matthew 27:3).

away sorrowful, but he didn't repent (Luke 18:23). It is not *regret*, simply wishing the deed had not happened. Pilate, who betrayed our Lord, washed his hands in regret over turning Christ over to the mob, but he didn't repent (Matthew 27:24). Repentance is not *resolve*. It is not like a New Year's resolution where we attempt to do something different. Nor is it *reform*, trying to turn over a new leaf. Judas took the thirty pieces of silver back to the priests. He reformed, but he didn't repent (Matthew 27:3).

Repentance is derived from a Greek word that literally means "to change one's mind." It sets off a chain reaction. It is a change of mind that affects a change of will, of volition, which then results in a change of action. If you are looking for the perfect illustration of this process, you can find it in the parable of the prodigal son recorded in Luke 15. The boy took his inheritance, left home, and headed for the bright lights of the big city where he squandered it all in sinful living. Broke and broken he landed a job feeding the swine in a filthy pig pen. Then, "he came to himself" (Luke 15:17). This change of mind brought about a change of his will. The next verse quotes him saying, "I will arise and go to my father." Once his mind and volition had truly changed, his actions soon followed: "He arose and came to his father" (Luke 15:20). Repentance is a change of mind. That is it. But if your mind is truly changed, your volition will be changed as well, resulting in a turnaround, a change of action.

Jesus promised us that if we do not change our minds about our self (we cannot save ourselves), our sin (it is not a little vice; it is so serious it necessitated the cross), and our Savior (He is not just some teacher or prophet but our sin bearer), then the end result is that we will perish. Which brings us to an important question. Where is repentance in the salvation experience? Does it precede faith? Or does faith have to come before repentance? The Bible teaches repentance and faith are both the gifts of God's grace. They are different sides of the same coin. Charles Spurgeon, author of the classic devotional *Morning and Evening*, says they are "[conjoined] twins . . . vitally joined together, born at the same time." Repentance alone will not get you to heaven. But you cannot get there without it. "Unless you repent, you will all likewise perish."

When all is said and done, what difference will it make if you drive the most expensive luxury car, fly around on private planes, wear designer clothing, eat vitamin-enriched foods, work out rigorously, sleep on a name-brand mattress, live in a mansion on the water, and are buried in a mahogany casket—only to stand in judgment to meet a God you do

not know? Not all of God's promises are for our well-being; some are sent with a warning. "Unless you repent you will all likewise perish." Change your mind . . . now!

— A PROMISE AND A PRAYER —

The goodness of God leads you to repentance.
ROMANS 2:4

Lord, thank You that You grant to me repentance and faith. Search my heart and see if there are any wicked ways in me. May Your goodness lead me to repentance. In Jesus' name, amen.

35 THE PROMISE OF RENEWAL

"If My people who are called by My name will humble
themselves, and pray and seek My face, and turn
from their wicked ways, then I will hear from heaven,
and will forgive their sin and heal their land."

—2 CHRONICLES 7:14

One way I have maintained peace in our home across these decades is by not mentioning what a fabulous cook my mother was during my childhood. In the early years of our marriage when the Thanksgiving dressing would come out of the oven in more liquid form than the gravy, I kept my mouth shut. Some time ago I was passing through the kitchen while Susie, my wife, was busy preparing the evening meal. My eyes fell on an old notecard that had yellowed through the years. Looking closely, I noted my mother's handwriting on it. It was an old recipe for one of my favorite dishes. When followed precisely as the directions said, Susie made a dish that tasted exactly like my mother used to make.

God has implanted within our hearts a longing for something more, a season of spiritual refreshing, a revival or renewal. He has His own recipe for revival and has recorded it in the Bible for each of us to follow: "If My people . . . will . . . then I will hear from heaven." And when His recipe

is followed as He wrote it and put into practice, it will enable us to soar into spiritual realms of blessing some of us have never known.

WHAT IS GOD'S DESIRE?

In following God's recipe for revival there are some vital questions that must be asked and properly answered. First, What is *God's desire*? He said, "If My people . . . then. . . ." God is waiting, willing, and longing to send a fresh wind of His Spirit on us. This is His desire. However, He did not make us to function as puppets, but as people. He loves us too much to overrule our own will. Consequently, while spiritual renewal is always a sovereign act of a holy God, there is also a sense in which it is conditional. "If My people. . . ." If certain conditions are met, certain results are sure to follow.

God longs to send a spirit of revival and renewal to His people. Peter reminded us that He is "not willing that any should perish" (2 Peter 3:9). There is a very real sense in which revival is not a miracle. It is simply God's promised response to conditions met by His people.

WHAT IS GOD'S DESIGN?

Another important question to be asked is, What is *God's design*? He has designed revival in such a fashion that it is

conditioned on God's own people. Listen to His invitation: "If *My* people . . ." Reading the history of God's visitation resulting in several "great awakenings" reveals they most often were ignited when one man or one woman became desperate for the fresh winds of the Spirit of God to blow on their life.

God's biggest problem today is not with the lost but with His own people. We are watching the rapid decay of a Western moral culture all around us while thinking it is rooted in the decline of a moral fabric with the accompanying influence of an increasingly secular and often downright godless ideology that has permeated our society. However, God reveals in this promise of renewal that His biggest problem is not with "them"; it is with "us." Or, as Jesus once opined, we should not be spending our effort trying to get a splinter out of someone else's eye when we have a two-by-four protruding out of our own (Matthew 7:3–5). God's design for revival begins with His own people—with you and me.

WHAT IS GOD'S DEMAND?

Next, we have the question, What is *God's demand*? It begins with a call to each of us to "humble ourselves," to recognize and confess our need to seek Him above all things. The Christian in search of revival must be on constant vigil to avoid the temptation of spiritual pride and self-centeredness.

True humility manifests itself in a "broken and a contrite heart" (Psalm 51:17) before the Lord.

Next, we are to "pray." Behind this word is not the idea of mere recitation of someone else's words, but an earnest and personal calling out to Him. Every true revival in history was ushered in on the wings of prayer. When we read the lives of the first-generation believers in the book of Acts, we find this truth on virtually every page.

We are to humble ourselves and pray, but there is more to this recipe. We are to "seek [His] face." If we spent as much time seeking His face today as some of us do seeking His hand for what we can get from Him, we would be well on the way to revival. When you arrive at the place where you love Him for who He is and not for what He may do for you, you will understand the promise that 2 Chronicles 7:14 provides for you.

Finally, God demands that we "turn from [our] wicked ways." Sin that is unconfessed, and therefore unforgiven, is the greatest obstacle to personal revival. Solomon reminded us, "He who covers his sins will not prosper, but whoever confesses and forsakes them will have mercy" (Proverbs 28:13). Forsaking your sin is a good indicator that you have truly confessed and repented, turned from your "wicked ways."

WHAT IS GOD'S DELIGHT?

Lastly, What is *God's delight*? Look at the last phrase of our promise: "I will hear from heaven, and will forgive their sin and heal their land." Nothing delights God more than this because it appropriates all that the cross of Christ involved. God delights more in healing our hearts and homes than we do ourselves.

While this promise of renewal is God's work, there is a very real sense it is conditioned on our response. Follow His recipe. Our part is not that difficult. Simply follow the directions. And then hold to His promise: "If My people. . . . then I will hear from heaven."

───────── **A PROMISE AND A PRAYER** ─────────

Humble yourselves in the sight of the Lord, and He will lift you up.
JAMES 4:10

Lord, You are beautiful. Your face is all I seek. And when Your eyes are on this child, Your grace abounds to me. In Jesus' name, amen.

36 THE PROMISE OF WISDOM

If any of you lacks wisdom, let him ask of God, who gives to all liberally and without reproach, and it will be given to him. But let him ask in faith, with no doubting, for he who doubts is like a wave of the sea driven and tossed by the wind. For let not that man suppose that he will receive anything from the Lord; he is a double-minded man, unstable in all his ways.

—JAMES 1:5–8

Many of us live today suffering from the consequences of bad decisions we made in the past. These decisions were made because when we arrived at some intersection of life needing to decide which way to turn, we turned the wrong way simply because of unwise decisions. Knowledge is the one thing that is not lacking in our modern culture today. Knowledge is exploding. Wisdom is what is lacking. There is a stark difference in the two. Knowledge is the accumulation of facts. Most of us can grow in knowledge if we stay in the library or in front of our computer screens long enough. Wisdom, however, is the ability to take the facts we have at hand and, using heavenly judgment, apply what we know to the earthly situations around us. And we have a promise from God: if we lack wisdom, we can pray, ask Him for it, and "it will be given" to us. There is a supernatural element at our disposal that is involved in our ability to make wise choices in life. Yet, sadly, prayer is often relegated to the back recesses of our minds when it comes time to make major decisions.

> Sadly, prayer is often relegated to the back recesses of our minds when it comes time to make major decisions.

Applying this supernatural wisdom was the point of Paul's prayer for the church at Ephesus. Paul asked "that the God of our Lord Jesus Christ, the Father of glory, may give to you the spirit of wisdom" (Ephesians 1:17). Stop a moment. Read that verse again. Wisdom is not simply God's promise to you, but it is His gift to you as well. This was also the point of Paul's prayer for the Colossians: "We . . . pray for you . . . that you may be filled with the knowledge of His will in all wisdom and spiritual understanding" (Colossians 1:9). Again, wisdom is God's gift to us if we would but ask for it.

In our modern, educated, and sophisticated fast-paced world, there has never been a time when we needed wisdom more than we do now. Our generation is more progressive than any that has come before. We fly higher and faster and travel farther. More of us have multi-graduate degrees than ever before. All around us knowledge is exploding. We accumulate data and store it in a way that would have been unfathomable in my father's generation. Technology is advancing so quickly that the latest and greatest computer gadgets are already outdated a few months after their release. Search engines like Google have put information and knowledge of the smallest detail from unknown places and sources instantly, within seconds, at our immediate disposal. Our modern world is filled with knowledge.

But, while knowledge continues to expand and tools for obtaining it become more and more advanced, wisdom is clearly lacking. Lives are in shambles. Families are broken. Suicide rates are at their highest. Millions of lives are snuffed out in abortion clinics before they ever have a chance to breathe their first breath. Evidence of Christian morality is at a record low. Our world is dark, violent, and constantly moving from one chaotic disaster to another. Wisdom is lacking everywhere, from the White House to our house. But God has left us a promise: "If any of you lacks wisdom, let him ask of God . . . and it will be given."

> While knowledge continues to expand and tools for obtaining it become more and more advanced, wisdom is clearly lacking.

To whom does God give this divine discernment? To those who ask. It comes from Him. It is His gift to us. How strange that so few of us simply ask God for this gift He so freely desires to give. We do not acquire wisdom from practical experience. We don't get it by sitting for years in the classroom. Wisdom comes from above; it is God's gift to us.

And His desire is to not just give it to you but to give it "liberally and without reproach" when you simply ask Him for it. Yet some of us who need wisdom the most seem to be too proud to ask for it. We can learn a lesson from the wisest man who ever lived, King Solomon, who contributed much to the book of wisdom we call Proverbs in our Bible. When, as a young man, he was on the brink of inheriting the kingdom from his father, King David, the Lord presented him with an incredible proposition: "Ask! What shall I give you?" (1 Kings 3:5). Solomon's response? "Give to Your servant an understanding heart to judge Your people, that I may discern between good and evil" (1 Kings 3:9). At that moment, Solomon could have asked God for anything. But he asked for what he knew he needed most—wisdom. And God gave it to him.

When we live without wisdom, life goes something like this: We try to cope with the circumstance ourselves. We call for another prescription drug. We make another appointment with our counselor. We order the latest self-help book. There is nothing wrong with any of that, but many of us consider prayer a last resort when all else has been tried. King David reminded us, "It is better to trust in the LORD than to put confidence in man" (Psalm 118:8).

But not everyone who asks for wisdom gets it. The Bible says we are to "ask in faith, with no doubting." Wisdom is

given to those who truly believe and ask in faith, for "without faith it is impossible to please Him" (Hebrews 11:6). Do you need wisdom? Then pray and ask . . . in faith . . . without doubting . . . and God will grant it to you "liberally." That is His promise to you. And He keeps His promises—all of them!

———— A PROMISE AND A PRAYER ————

The fear of the LORD is the beginning of wisdom.
PROVERBS 9:10

Lord, I need wisdom to get through this day, so I come before You now to take You at Your word and to believe Your promise by faith. Grant me this supernatural wisdom that I might honor You in all I do and say. In Jesus' name, amen.

37 THE PROMISE FOR THE FUTURE

*Now to Him who is able to keep you from stumbling, and
to present you faultless before the presence of His glory with
exceeding joy, to God our Savior, who alone is wise, be glory and
majesty, dominion and power, both now and forever. Amen.*

—JUDE VV. 24–25

*I*s it actually possible for a believer to stumble away
from the grace of God? You might have heard some
people use the phrase "falling from grace" to describe someone who has, in their view, departed from the faith and lost
their salvation. For the believer it is never a matter of falling
from grace. After all, grace is God's unmerited favor to begin
with and is not earned or deserved. The believer never falls
from grace, because the believer has fallen *into* grace. And
because of this truth the Bible promises that Christ is "able
to keep you from stumbling, and to present you faultless"
before His Father's throne.

This promise, with its abiding hope, is rooted in two
things: the sovereignty of God and the security of the
believer. Our God is sovereign. That is a big theological word
that simply means that God always does what He pleases and
is always pleased with what He does. And the good news is

that once we have placed our trust in Christ, He holds us securely in His hand—so much so that Jesus promised, "I give them eternal life, and they shall never perish; neither shall anyone snatch them out of My hand" (John 10:28).

THE SOVEREIGNTY OF GOD

Embedded in this promise God gives us through Jude is the assurance of the *sovereignty of God*. Jude began, "Now to Him who is able." He is able. No matter what the need might be, He is able to meet it. We are not talking about a God whose heroics are confined to bygone days. It is not that He *was* able. Nor are we talking about a God who is powerless to intervene on our behalf today but has bright hope for tomorrow. It is not that He *will be* able. He *is* able—this very minute. He was able in the past, He will be able in the future, but He is also able right now.

> He *is* able—this very minute. He was able in the past, He will be able in the future, but He is also able right now.

God's sovereignty is properly described with this phrase: "He is able." Our limitations of human language cannot begin to describe God's sovereignty. Jude made an attempt to express it with four words as he brought his small epistle to a swelling benediction. "Glory . . . majesty . . . Dominion . . . power." When we speak of His glory and His majesty, we are reminded He is *omniscient*. As Jude said, He "alone is wise." Dominion speaks of His *omnipresence*. He is everywhere present, and it is His kingdom that "rules over all" (Psalm 103:19). Power speaks of His *omnipotence*. All power and authority are His. Whatever your situation or circumstance, you have a God who "is able."

THE SECURITY OF THE BELIEVER

Also embedded in this promise is the assurance of the *security of the believer*. God makes plain that we are secure in the now life and also in the next life. We have security in the *now* life. He is able to "keep you from stumbling." It is wonderful to know that in some future day Christ is going to be able to present us before His Father in the next life, but it is equally wonderful to know that He is also able to keep us from falling in the now life.

When our family moved from the little Oklahoma county seat town of Ada to the huge and rapidly growing city center of Fort Lauderdale, Florida, our two daughters were only four and two years of age. In those early big-city days, we would get in the car, leaving home to drive to church or dinner, and were immediately confronted with massive traffic jams, long lines at traffic lights, and strange surroundings. Our oldest child became obsessed with a question. From the back seat of the car, she would bombard me with the same

> He is not only able to keep you from falling but to keep you from stumbling.

question: "We will be able to get home, won't we Daddy?" My answer was always the same reassuring words, "Yes, honey, I promise." It is really important for a child to know she can return to the safety and security of her own home. And it is important for a child of God as well to not have to wonder from day to day if they are saved or lost, but to have the promised assurance that God is able to hold us up and see us through. He is not only able to keep you from falling but to keep you from stumbling.

But there is more. We are secure in Christ not just in the now life but in the next life as well. He has promised to "present you faultless before the presence of His glory with exceeding joy." No one is "faultless" today. We all have our spots and blemishes brought about by wrong decisions along the way. But there is coming a day when we will be faultless; we will be like Him. The apostle John revealed, "It has not yet been revealed what we shall be, but we know that when He is revealed, we shall be like Him, for we shall see Him as He is" (1 John 3:2). Think of it. We shall be like Him—faultless to stand before the throne.

One day the Lord Jesus will have the joy of presenting His bride, the church, you and me, without spot or wrinkle to His Father. It was the anticipation of this joy that enabled

Him to endure the cross. The writer of Hebrews expressed it well, saying, "Jesus, the author and finisher of our faith, who for the joy that was set before Him endured the cross, despising the shame, and has sat down at the right hand of the throne of God" (Hebrews 12:2).

It is one thing to promise to keep us from falling and another to promise to present us faultless before His Father's throne with exceeding joy. Consumed with this amazing promise, Jude laid down his pen, and all that was left to say was, "Amen!" Yes, amen and amen. What God promises, He performs.

A PROMISE AND A PRAYER

"I give them eternal life, and they shall never perish;
neither shall anyone snatch them out of My hand."
JOHN 10:28

Lord, thank You for the confident assurance I have because You have promised that You are able to keep me in the secure grip of Your own hand. If faith was good enough to save me, it is good enough to live by. In Jesus' name, amen.

38 THE PROMISE TO ISRAEL

"I will bring back the captives of My people Israel; they
shall build the waste cities and inhabit them; they shall
plant vineyards and drink wine from them; they shall also
make gardens and eat fruit from them. I will plant them
in their land, and no longer shall they be pulled up from
the land I have given them, says the LORD your God."

—AMOS 9:14–15

One of the greatest tangible proofs that the Bible is true is the way prophecies are made and fulfilled and the way promises are made and kept. The most obvious of all these prophecies and promises are the ones God has made and kept with His chosen people, the Jews. No volume written about the promises of God would be complete without a review of the promises to the Jewish people and the Jewish state of Israel. If you are looking for proof that God will keep His promises, take a trip to Israel and observe the miracle of a people dispersed among the nations for almost two thousand years who have returned to the land of promise and made the desert bloom, and whose nation has against all odds reemerged as a world leader—just as God has promised.

Israel plays a prominent role in the plan of God. Not only did God use these people to give His Word to the world

(Romans 3:1–2), but the Jews were the vehicle He used to give His Son to the world as well (Romans 9). In our modern world, all eyes are on Israel. Pick up

In our modern world, all eyes are on Israel.

a newspaper or news magazine, scan the internet for world news, and you will find mention of Israel in some form or fashion. This little country, the size of the state of New Jersey, has, in many ways, become the center of world trouble just as the prophets prophesied and just as God promised. Keeping an eye on Israel keeps our finger on the pulse of world history and Bible prophecy.

Way back in the unfolding chapters of Genesis, God made a promise to Abraham, saying, "Get out . . . to a land that I will show you. I will make you a great nation . . . and in you all the families of the earth shall be blessed" (Genesis 12:1–3). Then the Lord enlarged on His promise of giving Israel a land, saying, "I will establish My covenant . . . for an everlasting covenant, to be God to you and your descendants . . . also I give to you and your descendants after you the land . . . as an everlasting possession; and I will be their God" (Genesis 17:7–8). God repeated His promise of the land not only to Abraham and his son Isaac but to Jacob as well: "The land on which you lie I will give to you and your descendants . . . and in you and in your seed all the families of the earth shall be blessed" (Genesis 28:13–14). God kept

His promise. Joshua led the children of Israel into the promised land and took possession of it.

Israel became a world power under the kingships of David and Solomon. But because they began to follow other gods, the kingdom was divided, and ultimately the Jews were taken into captivity by foreign nations. The holy city of Jerusalem was ravaged by the Romans, and the Jews were left without a land or a country. But what God had promised, He would perform in His own timing and His own way.

God had warned Israel He would not tolerate her worship of foreign gods. The Lord scattered the people among the nations, warning, "You will be left few in number among the nations where the LORD will drive you . . . you shall find no rest" (Deuteronomy 4:27; 28:65). True to His word, the Jewish people were scattered in AD 70 when Titus and his Roman legions destroyed Jerusalem. For two thousand years they lived as a despised and persecuted people without a land to call their own. One in three Jews in all the world were annihilated in Hitler's concentration camps. Against all odds these chosen people maintained their identity and

> Against all odds these chosen people maintained their identify and lived with the constant hope that they would celebrate their annual feasts "next year in Jerusalem."

lived with the constant hope that they would celebrate their annual feasts "next year in Jerusalem."

God promised there would come a day when He would regather the Jews from all over the four corners of the world, bring them back into their own land, and reestablish them as a nation. He promised, "I will take you from among the nations, gather you out of all countries, and bring you into your own land" (Ezekiel 36:24). And what He promised, He performed. On May 14, 1948, the United Nations took a vote that startled the world and recognized the reestablished state of Israel as a sovereign nation after two millennia of exile. Never in recorded history was a nation reborn in such a fashion. The ancient Hebrew language was restored, and in short time Israel grew to become a world power. Twenty-five hundred years earlier, through the prophet Isaiah, God had promised, "It shall come to pass in that day that the Lord shall set His hand again the second time to recover the remnant of His people . . . assemble the outcasts of Israel, and gather together the dispersed of Judah from the four corners of the earth" (Isaiah 11:11–12).

Today Israel is a thriving nation, blessing the world with its advanced scientific and medical research, leading the way in helping keep the world safe with one of the world's most sophisticated intelligence networks and powerful military structures, and bringing hope and help through its contributions to literature and the arts. Walk the streets of Jerusalem today and you will see Russian Jews who fled persecution and pogroms; dark-skinned Ethiopian Jews, descendants of Solomon and the Queen of Sheba; Sephardic Jews from the Arab world; and Ashkenazi Jews from Eastern Europe all blending together, just as God promised, into one nation, God's own chosen people. If you want to know if God keeps His promises, just look at Israel and the people we call the Jews. No wonder we call it *the promised land*!

A PROMISE AND A PRAYER

Now the LORD said to Abram . . . "I will bless you and make
your name great; and you shall be a blessing. I will bless
those who bless you, and I will curse him who curses you;
and in you all the families of the earth shall be blessed."
GENESIS 12:1–3

Lord, how blessed to see and know that You are faithful, that what You promise, You will always provide—in Your own way and in Your own timing. In Jesus' name, amen.

39 THE PROMISE OF HIS PRESENCE

"I am the Alpha and the Omega, the Beginning and the End," says the Lord, "who is and who was and who is to come, the Almighty."

—REVELATION 1:8

This promise in today's verse—that the Lord Jesus encompasses everything from beginning to end, from first to last—is such an important reminder that it is repeated several times in the book of Revelation. Since Alexander had conquered most of the Mediterranean world, the Greek language had become the universal written language of the age. The New Testament was originally delivered to us in this language. Consequently, the gospel spread rapidly in the first century without a language barrier. *Alpha* is the first of the twenty-four letters in the Greek alphabet. *Omega* is the last letter of the alphabet. When Jesus said, "I am the Alpha and the Omega, the Beginning and the End," it was His assurance to each of us that He is always with us, from the first breath we breathe until the last breath we take. But even more, it is His promise that He has existed from all eternity and in Him is all that can ever be.

The Revelation was written by the apostle John when he was exiled on the island of Patmos by the Roman government.

Immediately after quoting this promise of Jesus, he continued, "I, John . . . was on the island that is called Patmos for the word of God and for the testimony of Jesus Christ. I was in the Spirit on the Lord's Day" (Revelation 1:9–10). There is so much behind those words. Perhaps you feel like you are in the midst of a difficult situation yourself. Patmos was a desolate, barren, uninhabited rock of an island, ten miles long by six miles wide, just off the Asia Minor coast in the Aegean Sea. The Roman government used it as a sort of an Alcatraz, a place where they dumped hardened criminals from their conquered nations as well as those with severe mental disorders. It was like a zoo filled with wild human beings. John, over ninety years of age, was abandoned there by the Romans because he would not compromise the gospel message. As he testified, he was there "for the word of God and for the testimony of Jesus Christ."

> [Patmos] was like a zoo filled with wild human beings.

If ever anyone needed to hold to the promise that the Lord was in control, that He was the "Alpha and Omega," it was John. Listen to him closely: "I . . . was on the island that is called Patmos." But that is only half the story. He continued, "I was in the Spirit on the Lord's Day." Because Jesus is your Alpha and Omega, it is not where you are but *Whose* you are that matters most!

ON PATMOS WE SEE LIABILITIES

Look at John. Listen to him: "I . . . was on the island that is called Patmos." Talk about liabilities. Patmos was filled with them. The surroundings were adverse. The type of people with whom he associated posed a challenge. He had to scrounge for what food he could find. There was no safe place to sleep. And the sea . . . all he could see was the sea stretching endlessly in every direction.

Perhaps you are living on your own personal Patmos faced with all shapes and sizes of liabilities of your own. None of us are immune to Patmos and its liabilities.

> None of us are immune to Patmos and its liabilities.

But stop! Remember, that is only half the story. "I was in the Spirit on the Lord's Day." When he said that, his liabilities were turned into a reminder of lordship. Jesus had not abandoned His throne. He was the "Alpha and Omega." John saw a purpose in his being there under the lordship of Christ. From this unpleasant circumstance on Patmos, filled with its unique liabilities, God gave us the Apocalypse, the book of Revelation, through the pen of John.

You may be on your personal Patmos today faced with liabilities. But they can be translated into His lordship in your life. It is not *where* you are that matters most—it is *Whose* you are that really counts.

ON PATMOS WE SEE LIMITATIONS

Look at John. Listen to him: "I . . . was on the island that is called Patmos." Behind that phrase were limitations. Patmos was filled with them. Every morning he woke to see the sea. At night, sleeping in some cave, he watched the moonlight dancing on the waves. He was cut off, isolated, out of control. He could not sit with his friends, walk through the market-place, fellowship with the believers in church. He had none of his books. He heard no news from home. It is easy for us, as well, to fall into the "I was on the island that is called Patmos" syndrome, seeing only our liabilities and our limitations.

But stop! That is only half the story. Listen to John: "I was in the Spirit on the Lord's Day." When he declared this, his limitations gave way to liberty. He was free. He was no prisoner even if he was exiled on Patmos. Earlier Paul had said, "Where the Spirit of the Lord is, there is liberty" (2 Corinthians 3:17).

You may be on your personal Patmos today filled with your own unique limitations. But they can be lost in the liberty and freedom Christ brings. It is not *where* you are. It is *Whose* you are that matters most.

ON PATMOS WE SEE LONELINESS

Look at John. Listen to him: "I was on the island that is called Patmos." Behind those words was loneliness. There was no

one with whom to talk. He was the companion of a bunch of hard-hearted, embittered men. It is no wonder he later said of heaven that there "was no more sea" (Revelation 21:1). No more separation. No more liabilities, limitations, or loneliness. Some people today never get out of verse 9; they have eyes only for Patmos and put their focus there.

But stop! That is only half the story. John continues, "I was in the Spirit on the Lord's Day." When he said that, all his loneliness turned into love. Loneliness has its own way of being lost in the love of Christ when we lift our focus from our own Patmos and say with John, "I was in the Spirit on the Lord's Day."

Jesus Christ is your "Alpha and Omega." He is the beginning of all things and is with you through it all . . . and forever. Hold to His promise and remember: it is not *where* you are that matters most. It is *Whose* you are that turns your loneliness into love.

A PROMISE AND A PRAYER

For by Him all things were created that are in heaven and that are on earth, visible and invisible, whether thrones or dominions or principalities or powers. All things were created though Him and for Him. And He is before all things, and in Him all things consist.
COLOSSIANS 1:16–17

Lord, nothing can happen to me that takes You by surprise. You are my Alpha and my Omega. Help me remember today it is not where I am but Whose I am that matters most. In Jesus' name, amen.

40

THE PROMISE OF HIS RETURN

"If I go and prepare a place for you, I will come again and receive
you to Myself, that where I am, there you may be also."

—JOHN 14:3

*I*t may well be that the greatest chasm between the first-
century church and the modern twenty-first-century
church is in the very way we respond to this promise of Christ
to "come again." His promised return is virtually a forgotten
subject in our more sophisticated Sunday gatherings. When
was the last time you remember hearing a message on the second coming of Christ, this coming great and climactic event
in all of human history? Yet His return was constantly on
the minds and lips of the early believers. The New Testament
writers referred to the second coming of Christ more than
any other single subject, prominently mentioning it with
more than three hundred references. There was a word that
constantly escaped the lips of these first-generation believers. *Maranatha!* It literally means, "the Lord is coming."
They greeted each other with this word. They comforted one
another with this word. This is the word they shouted across
the cursing crowds to their friends dying on crosses of execution for their faith and burning at the stakes of martyrdom.

They arose every single morning and pillowed their heads every single night living with expectation, looking for, and eagerly anticipating their soon-coming King.

In today's church, talk of future prophecies on God's timetable of the last days draws raised eyebrows, rolled eyes, and wide and verbal yawns. When we lose our expectation and our hope in the future, we resort to having no power in the present. We lament today's lack of evangelistic fervor and passion for reaching those without Christ. But it is often the result of a loss of the sense of urgency that comes in living in anticipation of Christ's any-minute return. It also can result in an alarming lack of holiness and personal purity as, increasingly, life is lived with little to no urgency in being ready to meet the Lord in that unknown moment when He comes again.

The Bible has the promise of three major comings laced throughout its pages. First is the coming of Christ, born of a virgin in the tiny, obscure village of Bethlehem. He came and "dwelt among us" (John 1:14) for thirty-three years. Next, there is the coming of the Holy Spirit foretold primarily by the prophet Joel. This coming took place on the day of Pentecost when the Holy Spirit came to indwell believers with the promise to never leave or forsake us, empowering us for service. And now, the only major coming yet to be fulfilled is the second coming of the Lord Jesus. Just as surely as He came the first time, He is coming again for His bride, the church. And when He comes, we who are alive "shall be caught up together with them in the clouds to meet the Lord in the air. And thus we shall always be with the Lord" (1 Thessalonians 4:17). We have and hold to His precious promise: "I will come again."

When Christ does return, it will be with great power and glory. Handel's classic masterpiece, the "Hallelujah" chorus, captures the sense of joy and glory John described in the Revelation: "The kingdoms of this world have become the kingdoms of our Lord and of His Christ, and He shall reign forever and ever" (Revelation 11:15). The greatest fact of Bible prophecy is that Jesus Christ, faithful to His promise, is coming back visibly, bodily, and personally to this earth. Palm Sunday was not the last journey Jesus will ever make down the western slope of the Mount of Olives, across the Kidron Valley, and through the Eastern Gate of the city. He is coming back, and He won't be riding a donkey next time. Our conquering King will be mounted on a white stallion as He returns to His Holy City.

The entire Bible testifies of Jesus' promised return. The angels foretold it as He ascended back into heaven after the resurrection, "Men of Galilee, why do you stand gazing up into heaven? This same Jesus, who was taken up from you into heaven, will so come in like manner as you saw Him

go into heaven" (Acts 1:11). Paul spoke of Christ's return when instructing us pertaining to the Lord's Supper: "For as often as you eat this bread and drink this cup, you proclaim the Lord's death till He comes" (1 Corinthians 11:26). And the night before His own execution, Jesus promised, "I will come again and receive you to Myself" (John 14:3). Woven as a thread throughout the Scriptures is the hope that Jesus Christ will come again, first to rapture His church, and then after a period of tribulation, to set up His earthly kingdom from the throne of David in Jerusalem to reign and rule for a period of perfect peace and then to usher in the endless ages of eternity.

The last promise of the entire Bible comes from the lips of our Lord: "Surely I am coming quickly" (Revelation 22:20). While there are thousands of promises in the Bible, the promise of the second coming of Christ is the major promise yet to be fulfilled, marking the climax of all of human history. Just as surely as His other promises have been fulfilled, so will His promise to come again.

The last prayer recorded in the Bible is also a request for Christ to return. Exiled on the island of Patmos by the Romans, John, having heard the promise of Jesus to return, burst out into prayer, "Even so, come, Lord Jesus!" (Revelation 22:20). Just five words. So often the most powerful prayers are short ones like this, as John anticipated seeing

Christ return in great glory and going with Him to heaven, where time would be no more.

Before you finish this chapter, take a moment to examine your own life. Are you ready to meet Him? What if it were today? He keeps His promises—all of them. Join John now and pray, "Even so, come, Lord Jesus."

A PROMISE AND A PRAYER

Behold, He is coming with clouds, and every eye
will see Him, even they who pierced Him.
REVELATION 1:7

Lord, it may be a morn when the day is awaking and sunlight is breaking through shadows and darkness that You will come in the fullness of glory to receive from the world Your own. Even so, come, Lord Jesus. In Jesus' name, amen.

EPILOGUE

*W*e have come once again to the end of a volume. It may be that while you have been journeying through these pages, God's Spirit has been nudging you to believe His promises and to put your faith and trust in Christ for the forgiveness of your sin and receive God's free promise of eternal life. After all, heaven is God's personal and free gift to you. It cannot be earned, neither is it ever deserved. We are all sinners, and each and every one of us has fallen short of God's perfect standard for our lives. God is a God of love, but He is also a God of justice and, therefore, must punish sin. This is where Jesus steps in. He is the holy and sinless God-man who came to take your own sins on Himself and die on the cross in your place as punishment for those sins. But just knowing this fact it not enough. You must transfer your trust from your own human effort to Christ alone, placing your faith in Him.

If you would like to receive this free gift of eternal life right now, it is yours for the asking. One of the most pointed and precious promises in all the Bible is found in Romans 10:13: "Whoever calls on the name of the LORD shall be saved." Believe it and you can join Simon Peter in his prayer on the Sea of Galilee. Say it: "Lord, save me!" (Matthew

14:30). The following is a suggested prayer you can pray, right now, from your own heart, no matter where you are.

> *Dear Lord Jesus,*
> *I know I have sinned. I know that, in and of myself,*
> *I do not deserve eternal life. Please forgive me for my*
> *sin. Thank You for taking my sin on Your own body*
> *and dying on the cross on my behalf and in my place.*
> *I believe Your promise that by calling on You I can be*
> *saved. I trust in You as the only One who can save me*
> *from an eternity of being separated from a holy God.*
> *Come into my life. Lord, save me. I accept Your free*
> *and gracious offer of forgiveness, abundant life, and*
> *eternal life with You.*

Now, as an expression of the fact that you believe God is not a liar and will keep His promises, say, "Thank You, Lord, for coming into my life this very moment as my very own personal Lord and Savior."

A simple prayer cannot save you. But Jesus can . . . and will. After all, He promised! If this prayer has expressed the desire of your heart, you can now claim another of the promises Jesus made to those who believe in Him: "Most assuredly . . . he who believes in Me has everlasting life" (John 6:47).

You can now join millions of Christ's followers who stand on and believe His scriptural promise from John: "These things I have written to you who believe in the name of the Son of God, that you may know that you have eternal life, and that you may *continue to* believe in the name of the Son of God" (1 John 5:13).

Now, don't keep these promises all to yourself. What good is good news if you don't share it? Tell someone of your newfound faith in Him.

MISSION:DIGNITY

*A*ll the author's royalties and any additional proceeds from the Code series (including *The Promise Code*) go to the support of Mission:Dignity, a ministry that enables thousands of retired ministers (and, in most cases, their widows) who are living near the poverty level to live out their days with dignity and security. Many of them spent their ministries in small churches that were unable to provide adequately for their retirement. They also lived in church-owned parsonages and had to vacate them upon their vocational retirement as well. Mission:Dignity tangibly shows these good and godly servants they are not forgotten and will be cared for in their declining years.

All the expenses for this ministry are paid out of an endowment that has already been raised. Consequently, anyone who gives to Mission:Dignity can be assured that every cent of their gift goes straight to one of these precious saints in need.

Find out more by visiting www.missiondignity.org or call toll-free 877-888-9409.

ABOUT THE AUTHOR

O. S. Hawkins is a graduate of TCU (BBA) and Southwestern Seminary (MDiv, PhD). For more than twenty years, he served pastorates at the First Baptist Church in Fort Lauderdale, Florida, and in Dallas, Texas. He is president of GuideStone Financial Resources, which serves 250,000 pastors, church staff, missionaries, doctors, and other workers of various Christian organizations with assets under management of more than $20 billion. He is the author of more than fifty books, including *The Joshua Code* and *The Jesus Code* and the entire Code series, with over two million copies sold. He preaches regularly at Bible conferences, evangelism conferences, and churches across the nation.

DRAW CLOSER TO GOD

*Y*ou'll understand Jesus' presence in the Old Testament in a new way as you journey with Pastor O. S. Hawkins through the Bible in *The Bible Code*. As Jesus revealed to the two disciples on the road to Emmaus, He can be found "in all the Scriptures" (Luke 24:27). And as we learn to find Jesus in every verse, we realize His constant presence in our lives as well.

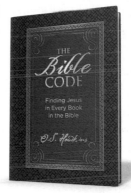

ISBN: 978-1-4002-1780-9

THOMAS NELSON
Since 1798